ENGAGING YOUTH IN LEADERSHIP DEVELOPMENT

Lesego Shibambo • Odily Díaz
Kat Wood • Thiago Nieman Ambrósio
Cameron Batkin • Phil Starr

CREDITS
Authors: Kenny Wade, Lesego Shibambo, Odily Díaz, Kat Wood, Thiago Nieman Ambrósio, Cameron Batkin, Phil Starr

Book and Series Editor: Lisa Aparicio

Copy Editors: Hailey Teeter, Emily Reyes, and Emily Knocke

Cover Design: Christian Cardona

Original Content Translators: Samuel Aparicio (Chapter 2), Everton Morais (Chapter 4)

TABLE OF CONTENTS

ABOUT THIS SERIES

"How do you guide youth to be confident in evangelism?"

"What should I be thinking about to make sure my youth are growing in their faith?"

"Sometimes I don't feel like I know what I'm doing as a leader. How am I going to help my youth develop their own leadership skills?"

We frequently hear questions like these from youth leaders all around the world. They are youth leaders in small churches and large churches. They are formally trained youth pastors and lay volunteer youth workers. Maybe you've asked questions like these as well.

This three-book series is our way of reaching out to local youth leaders to encourage and equip you in the deeply meaningful work you are doing. The challenge is that youth ministry is diverse, with ever-changing cultural nuances to navigate. Thus, we have chosen to focus each of these books on one of our core strategies in NYI — evangelism (BE), discipleship (DO), and leadership development (GO). These core strategies have served youth ministry in the Church of the Nazarene well since its earliest days. We have also invited in a diverse team of writers to help us share a balanced perspective with you. We trust you will enjoy this blend of voices and that the mix of perspectives will provide connection to your ministry setting no matter what your context.

Wherever you find yourself in ministry, know that you are appreciated, that you are prayed for, and that you bring more skills to youth ministry than you know.

May God bless you.

Gary Hartke
Director, Nazarene Youth International

PREFACE

When we talk about evangelism (BE), discipleship (DO), and leadership development (GO), it is generally easier for us to access voices similar to our own — ones who share ideas and strategies we are already familiar with. However, we believe that our three core strategies in Nazarene Youth International deserve a more nuanced discussion. We started this conversation in 2013 with a renewed emphasis on our core strategies and started talking about BE, DO, and GO.

Evangelism:
BE God's light, even in the dark places of our world.

Discipleship:
DO the hard work of becoming more like Jesus as you walk with others.

Leadership Development:
GO out into your community and learn as a servant leader.

As the conversation of BE, DO, and GO spread, we wanted to help the lessons emerging from those conversations to spread as well. We wanted the lessons to be taught by diverse voices, each bringing a unique perspective to the global conversation. To accomplish this, we needed a global team of writers and the result was this series which we believe is a true expression of what it means to be a global church.

We trust that you will benefit greatly from these diverse authors. A brief introduction for each one is provided at the beginning of their chapter. As you read, you will be reminded of the diversity of our church, not only through the content, but even in little ways, such as spelling. We have made the intentional choice to keep the vocabulary and spelling style for each author consistent with what is used in their part of the world. When a chapter has been translated from a different language, the spelling and vocabulary are more reflective of the translator's home country.

May God bless you in your ministry as you seek to actively engage your youth in evangelism, discipleship, and leadership development. We believe these books are starting points to help you move forward in your ministry with more intentionality. Where will you go from here? We invite you to take your place in the global story of BE, DO, and GO.

Lisa Aparicio
Editor
Ministry Development Coordinator, Nazarene Youth International

ACKNOWLEDGMENTS

The formation of a global writing team required the input and support of many individuals. It began with an invitation for all of our regional youth coordinators to share names with us of youth leaders from their region who excelled in evangelism, discipleship, or leadership development. Without the support and discernment of Ronald Miller (Africa Region), Janary Suyat de Godoy (Asia-Pacific Region), Diego Lopez (Eurasia Region), Milton Gay (Mesoamerica Region), Jimmy De Gouveia (South America Region), and Justin Pickard (USA/Canada Region) these books wouldn't have happened.

Video conference calls were hosted with all of the 18 writers to share, collaborate, and ultimately shape the structure of these books. The calls were organized and led by Shannon Greene (Global NYI Office). Her overall contribution to this project was absolutely invaluable. Kenny Wade (Youth in Mission) also participated in each call to share the background of the BE, DO, GO initiative. The context he provided gave the whole project a solid foundation to build on. Kenny also contributed to the series as the author of the introductions.

Ultimately though, these books wouldn't have been possible without the hard work of each of our writers. They have shared from their hearts about how they see God at work through the church's efforts to engage youth in evangelism, discipleship, and leadership development.

Africa
Wesley Parry (Evangelism)
Nicholas Barasa (Discipleship)
Lesego Shibambo
(Leadership Development)

Asia-Pacific
Daniel Latu (Evangelism)
Bakhoh Jatmiko (Discipleship)
Cameron Batkin
(Leadership Development)

Eurasia
Wouter van der Zeijden (Evangelism)
Nabil Habiby (Discipleship)
Kat Wood (Leadership Development)

Mesoamerica
Dario Richards (Evangelism)
Milton Gay (Discipleship)
Odily Díaz (Leadership Development)

South America
Christiano Malta (Evangelism)
Jaime Román Araya (Discipleship)
Thiago Nieman Ambrósio
(Leadership Development)

USA/Canada
Denise Holland (Evangelism)
Andrea Sawtelle (Discipleship)
Phil Starr (Leadership Development)

INTRODUCTION

Kenny Wade

Kenny Wade serves as the Youth in Mission Coordinator. Kenny believes youth ministry helps us think creatively about what it means for God's kingdom to come here on earth as we minister alongside youth whose lives are committed to Christ. He believes leaders are developed as they pioneer the way forward with the faith community, and the church is shaped as we go together.

Leadership development is an art form happening on the GO. It is a journey of following Jesus fully, lived within the accountability of community. Christ-following leaders are often formed along the way and are always in the process of learning. Success while on the GO can be measured in depth of relationship and in the transforming grace of God at work in you and in others (1 Timothy 4:11-16). Having a teachable spirit in the posture we have toward our own personal development and well-being will critically impact the longevity of our calling to GO.

My friendship with Bobby (which I shared about in the introductions for the BE and DO books) has been a very formative journey of leadership development while on the GO. Bobby and I met in our local community on the sidelines of our sons' sporting events. After stopping by Bobby's house at the end of the season, our friendship continued. Doing life with Bobby at his pace through coffee and conversation further developed me as a disciple. Our friendship was greatly impacted by my family's call and obedience to move away and GO where the Lord was directing us as volunteer missionaries in another country. This initiated an even deeper conversation of trust with Bobby and my trusting Bobby back to the Lord. We continued our friendship by the occasional video chat. All through our friendship, the Lord has been teaching me on the GO. This has led to my deepening trust in Christ to assume He is already at work in my neighbor and to attend to the hard work of holistic self-care; all while seeking to live in a posture of "sentness" wherever we GO.[1]

Jesus said that everything hangs on this: loving God with all we are and our neighbor as ourselves (Mark 12:28-34). As is the custom of the Kingdom, we must begin at the end — with self. If you GO but don't know how loved you are as a child of God, made in His image, then how can you lead others? This identity as the beloved is the holy vocation we are all born to fulfill as we are in the process of being renewed in the image of Christ, by the power of His Spirit at work in us.[2]

You can try to lead out of your own sense of identity and ability. The problem is, if you manage to lead, you probably won't be doing it very well or in the best way for God's kingdom to break into our world. One of my mentors has taught me that, from their experience, the discipline of self-leadership is often the very last area to be developed in the life of a leader. I will often give myself a pass on self-care with the false "higher calling" of attending to all the needs of others being met before my own basic need to BE with Christ and DO what He asks of me.

This is not what Jesus did. He invested 30 years of private preparation getting ready for three years of public ministry and mission. This stands in contrast to most models of ministry. We prepare for two to four years to serve for 30 to 50 years (Mark 6:1-12). Jesus escaped the turmoil of the day and the onslaught of the crowd to attune His whole person to the heartbeat of His Father (Luke 6:12). He defied expectations and accomplished the tasks of His calling in unexpected and slow ways. The leadership model we see of Christ on the GO with His disciples began with His own personal sense of identity as the beloved Son of God. (Matthew 3:17). Is that where we start?

We usually get the worshipping-God and loving-our-neighbor bits prioritized on our better days. But do we, with equal determination, pursue the nurturing of our whole person as we are created to do? To walk with Christ (BE) will result in living out the Gospel (DO), which leads to engaging in the mission (GO). This is dependent upon our tenacity to continually soak ourselves in the grace and goodness of God's presence. If we develop all areas of our lives but neglect the mastery of self-care, it will show. Mentally. Emotionally. Physically. Spiritually. Relationally. Professionally.

Jesus escaped the turmoil of the day and the onslaught of the crowd to attune His whole person to the heartbeat of His Father.

Taking advantage of educational opportunities provided to help develop us as Christ-following leaders is important. Technology gives us a huge advantage. I once video chatted from the northwest United States with my brother working in a remote refugee camp in the Horn of Africa. From the Nazarene Theological College in Brisbane, Australia, I took a live-video course on Psalms and Proverbs as part of a class at Nazarene Theological College in Manchester, England. I have participated and led in field training by video conference. I even dropped in on General Assembly voting by streaming video. I have connected with and been encouraged by friends in Christ on six continents! Leadership development is limited only by our imagination.

The greatest lessons we offer derive from non-verbal cues. Most of our leadership comes from the default posture of our lives more than the activities associated with our post or position. So how are we leading those we oversee? By loving God and others as we love ourselves? Does that mean God and others are getting the leftovers or the first fruits? These are tough and confronting questions leaders on the GO must ask themselves and then begin to develop within themselves before asking them of those who follow.

Good leading is good following.[3] Quality leaders can lead in various ways and allow the strengths and gifts of others to shine in the Kingdom. This participatory leadership can be practiced many different ways through the mission of the local church on the GO. God has always been calling His followers to GO out from where they are to where God wants them to be and do what God asks them to DO. This invitation to GO can be local, global, or both! God sent Jesus. Jesus sent His followers. God calls and sends us. Good leadership development happens in a posture of sentness, whether in our own neighbourhood or across creation (John 1:1-5,14). We are always on the GO as leaders on a journey of development. Always being sent. In progress. Growing in grace. Living in a posture of sentness in Christ requires vigilant dependence on God's provision and strength. Leaders GO when sent and trust God for the equipping, timing, and results (Matthew 10). Leadership development is meant to occur while we live in a posture of being "sent" and choose to be obedient and faithful.

Living in a posture of sentness in Christ requires vigilant dependence on God's provision and strength.

Back to my friend Bobby. A couple nights before we moved away, Bobby and I went out for pie and were gone until the early morning hours, talking through life and the faith journey together. God was sending my family and me as volunteer missionaries to another country through our church globally, but the Lord had taught me how to be the church missionally, embracing our sentness alongside my friend and his family locally. Maybe for Bobby's growth, and for mine, we needed to be apart. If Jesus was going to be real for Bobby and Bobby was going to trust Jesus, then they needed to journey together, and any temptation of co-dependence between Bobby and I had to be removed. The Lord continues to lead and guide both of our developments as we allow Him to work in our lives.

Leaders are called to BE and DO whatever it takes to develop, grow, and GO! I believe if we claim to be disciples of Jesus, then we are missionaries right where God has sent or placed us. God calls all followers of Christ to

When God calls us out of our comfort zones and asks us to give up everything, it is an all-or-nothing request.

be "missionaries" right where they are seeking to join Him in His already and ongoing mission. The most difficult place to be a Christ-following leader can be with our families, in our homes, around our churches, in our own neighbourhoods, communities, cultures, and contexts. When God calls us out of our comfort zones and asks us to give up everything, it is an all-or-nothing request (Matthew 19:16-30). Either all we are and have belongs to Him, or nothing does. Kingdom leaders are formed on the GO as we join God's mission in creative ways as we are discipled while we DO the same with others, and as we choose to BE with Christ. So ... GO!

CHAPTER 1

Biblical Foundations of Leadership Development

Lesego Shibambo

Lesego Shibambo serves as a pastor in Johannesburg, South Africa. Youth ministry is exciting to him because he is able to walk alongside young people who are flourishing in the love of Christ. Leadership development is important to Lesego because it is at the forefront of God's purpose for us to be transformed into His image.

Throughout history, leadership has been a popular and sought-out topic. Humans have always been interested in governing, leading, or shepherding people in one way or form. Societies have looked for and elevated people with some sort of knowledge, power, or charisma to lead them out of economical, political, physical, or social predicaments that have afflicted people throughout the centuries and around the world. We desire leaders who will alleviate challenges our societies face. We want someone to up-lift and empower us to move mountains and bring up generations to look forward to a better future. How long must we hunger and thirst for such leaders?

One of the many definitions of leadership is the ability to guide people or an organization toward a desired goal or way.[1] Working from this definition, leadership is made up of ability, guiding people, and finally having a des-tination or desired goal. In this chapter, we are going to take a look at what the Bible teaches us about these three components.

Leadership Takes Ability

You can go to your local bookstore or visit a website to purchase the latest books, tapes, or seminars on leadership by any number of world-famous authors, but at the end of the day you may feel overwhelmed, confused, or even pressured to seek some sort of instant leader-in-an-hour formula. This overabun-

People in leadership capacities seem to struggle to believe that they actually have the gift or ability to lead.

dance of resources for leaders attests to the great demand for them. People in leadership capacities seem to struggle to believe that they actually have the gift or ability to lead. One of the many gifts that Paul lists within Romans 12:8 is in fact *leadership*. If this is true, why is there such a disconnect? Let's break down some common misconceptions we have about leadership that may keep people from maximizing their leadership potential.

Culture Says, "Leaders Look Like Superheroes"

The influence of media on society has done an injustice to the idea of leadership. Pictures and scenes bombard us with the image of the hero saving the world, the one single person who is destined to fight off the bad guy. It's definitely entertaining, but the subliminal message is that only certain people are destined to become leaders. We grow up believing only certain people are born at the right time, under the right circumstances, and with all the right leadership skills they need. Even with all the resources and opportunities to help individuals become leaders, they are futile because the people using them believe they were not born with the leadership "gene" that has been passed down from generation to generation.

God Says, "You Were Created By the Creator"

"Then God said, 'Let us make humanity in our image to resemble us so that they may take charge of the fish of the sea, the birds in the sky, the livestock, all the earth, and all the crawling things on earth.'" (Genesis 1:26 CEB)

I have a genuine love for guitars. I know when I pick up a certain guitar, just by looking at the brand, I am in store for a world of sweet-sounding goodness. It's the same way you'd look at a BMW logo and brace yourself for some world-class German VA-VA-vroom on the accelerator pedal. It's all in the brand, right? The Fender guitar and the BMW car are products that belong to a particular manufacturer. Now, walk up to that BMW, open up the hood of the car, get really low, and begin to ask it in a tender voice *"Why were you made?"* No answer? How about raising your voice? That's always useful right? Maybe you talk to cars on the occasional bad day to take the stress away, but hopefully I would not catch any one of you actually doing that. The best way to find out about the product is to ask the producer, because they had a purpose and blueprint of all its specifications, its purpose, its life-span, its guarantee, and its limits — all down to the smallest bolt.

Unfortunately, this is how we approach leadership. We spend so much time asking the created about its purpose, ability, and how it's going to reach its potential. Instead, what we need to do is go back to the Creator, the One who rolled up the blueprint and began to create us with purpose, creativity, and excellence. The product apart from the producer is just an object without purpose.[2]

Read the verses from Genesis again, quoted at the beginning of this section. That's the blueprint right there. Here we have the details of what the created being will look like: "Let us make humanity in our image." The specs of humanity: God's likeness. The purpose of humanity: responsibility for the fish of the sea, the birds in the sky, the livestock, all the Earth, and all the crawling things on Earth. The place where humanity will be operational: the Earth. Finally, and most importantly, the created human is signed and delivered by the Creator, God. Before we can be effective, our purpose must be known.

God is the ultimate leader, and we have been made in God's image. However, shortly after God created us, we encountered someone who was intimidated by the purpose for which we had been created. He went so far as to manipulate the wording in the "do not do" section of our instructions for life. We didn't follow God's plan, and sin came in and distorted our purpose and capability to be like our Creator. Even so, God reached out to redeem us and remind us of our God-given purpose.

The Bible offers us many examples of individuals whose purpose seemed to be lost along the way, yet God continued to call and use them for the purposes of God's kingdom. For example:

Moses was the son of a Hebrew slave girl (being Hebrew was basically an automatic qualification for being a slave), was educated under the Egyptians, was a murderer, a shepherd, and wasn't called to be a leader until he was 40 years old. He couldn't speak well, and he had anger issues. Nonetheless, Moses is considered one of the greatest leaders of all time.[3]

Joseph had older brothers who hated him so much that they sold him as a slave. He was falsely jailed as an adulterer and forgotten in jail. God continued to work in his life and even helped him interpret dreams that led Joseph to become the second in command in Egypt.

David started life as a shepherd boy and later served as the king's private musician. He became king himself, but his reign was tainted by adultery and murder. Even so, David is later known as a man after God's own heart.

You see? We are not all the same, and we're certainly imperfect, but in the hands of the Creator, these leaders were brought to heights and were written about within the memoirs of history. Their purpose came from the Creator, and they were uniquely gifted to accomplish them. This leads us to a second myth.

Culture Says, "Leaders Have a Certain Personality"

Let me be honest here, I may be the guiltiest when it comes to this one. When leadership is mentioned, you may think of a specific type of person — someone who is good-looking, outspoken, tall, educated, well-mannered, an overachiever, popular, with over 70K Instagram followers. This image of a good leader is an outgoing extrovert who seems to have the power to win over a crowd with just a couple of words, no matter where they are. They're always in the spotlight, well dressed, and adored. There are always those individuals who seem to stand out, and the term "leader" is naturally associated with them because they do the very things that "ordinary" folk may tend to stay away from.

God Says, "You Are Uniquely Gifted"

"Now these are the gifts Christ gave to the church: the apostles, the prophets, the evangelists, and the pastors and teachers." (Ephesians 4:11 NLT)

Remember the above-mentioned leaders from the Bible? Imagine Moses, Joseph, and David all in the same room. To set the stage, picture that it's a black-tie party, the reunion class of the Old Testament leaders. If you had to choose, who would you follow? In your opinion, who is the leader you would want to rally behind? In one corner stands the mature and wise Moses, who even has his own spokesperson. In the other is Joseph, dressed up in silk and up-to-date with timepieces straight from Egypt. In another corner is the handsome David, walking humbly with a chalice in his big, mighty hands. It should be easy, right? My point is that any of them would be the right choice. Each of them has their strengths and weaknesses, and they each bring unique contexts and experiences to their leadership.

This earth would be so boring if people looked the same, talked the same, and offered the same gifting and talents. The earth would be unbearable if there were only one type of leader. Sure, there is a place for the extroverted socialite conqueror; they look good, and they're great at what they do. But there is also a place for the individual who enjoys being lost within the crowd and has influence over people in a more subtle way. Each person brings their own personality and capabilities, and we are stronger and better because of it.

God's plan and purpose is so vast. He has gifted leaders with a large range of talents and abilities. The verse quoted from Ephesians at the beginning of this section affirms this diversity. We can also read similar lists with even more descriptors in Romans 12:6-8 and 1 Corinthians 12:8-11. Search, find, and talk to God concerning all He laid within you, because it has a place and it has a purpose.

Culture Says, "You Should Lead From the Top Down"

CEO? Leader. Master chef? Leader. Principal? Leader. Pastor? I call double leader on that one! The assumption is that you can only find leaders at the top floor. In other words, the real leaders are the ones sitting behind a huge table with the big special chair. Leaders are either changing the world as they stroll down the street with masses following behind them, or they are in their big office writing up the plan to do that the very next day. Leaders can only be leaders if they have people who report to them, and they are leading from the top down.

God Says, "The Least is the Greatest"

"But Jesus called them to him and said, 'You know that the rulers of the Gentiles lord it over them, and their great ones exercise authority over them. It shall not be so among you. But whoever would be great among you must be your servant, and whoever would be first among you must be your slave, even as the Son of Man came not to be served but to serve, and to give his life as a ransom for many.'" (Matthew 20:25-28 ESV)

The scene within this passage has to be one of my top five most memorable moments of Jesus' ministry. It is here where the mother of two of Jesus' closest disciples, James and John, inquired about securing prestigious positions for them in the Messiah's kingdom. James and John's mother basically approached Jesus with a proposal: "Pssht! Hey Lord, you see my sons over there? Wouldn't the two of them be perfect to be your left- and right-hand men when you become king over the land?" The myth of the top-down leadership was so set in the mind of James and John's mother that it moved her to pursue some sort of arrangement guaranteeing a noteworthy and honorable future for her sons. The truth is that James and John became great leaders in the Church, so this isn't a discussion about their skill. However, Jesus' response set in motion a type of leadership His disciples would embrace, and it would change the face of the world. Jesus' life and teaching introduced His disciples to *servant* leadership. Robert K. Greenleaf, who coined the phrase "servant leadership," says, "The servant-leader is servant first... It begins with the natural feeling that one wants to serve, to serve first." Greenleaf writes:

> "A servant-leader focuses primarily on the growth and well-being of people and the communities to which they belong. While traditional leadership generally involves the accumulation and exercise of power by one at the 'top of the pyramid', servant leadership is different. The servant leader shares power, puts the needs of others first, and helps people develop and perform as highly as possible."[4]

Leadership as Guidance

The second part of our leadership definition asserts guiding people as a key aspect of leadership. The typical view of leadership can be seen as the "chosen one" up in front while the followers flock behind the leader. The expectation is that the leader has an endless well of insight, the right words at the right time, and an overall natural North Star internally guiding them. There is just one problem here: what happens when the leader fails or does not live up to the expectations of their followers? What happens if the leader does not have all the answers to all of the pressing matters that haunt the minds of the followers and oppress them in society? This unhealthy dependency on leaders can be seen by a simple click of a button on your television remote. A true leader, however, doesn't lead in order to hoard power and be served. True leadership, as modeled by Christ, is focused on guiding oneself first and eventually guiding one's followers to become leaders. Let's consider three factors to leadership as guidance.

Jesus' life and teaching introduced His disciples to *servant* leadership.

A leader first seeks to guide themselves.

Do you recall a certain New Testament, new-school, rugged leader who boldly proclaimed, "follow my example, as I follow the example of Christ" (1 Corinthians 11:1)? There is such an important leadership principle found within this short but powerful statement. Leaders do not seek followers; they seek to guide themselves, their own lives, and their own character. They lead from an example that they are truly living themselves. People follow because they are drawn to the authenticity and trustworthiness of such a leader.

A leader guides from the heart.

We are still conversing on the biblical foundations of leadership, and the primary biblical concern regarding a leader is the character of the heart of a leader. The word *heart* looked at from the Hebrew context was believed to be the "central and unifying organ of personal life. It was the innermost spring of an individual life, within the recesses of the heart dwelt the thoughts, plans, attitudes, fears, and hopes, which determined the character of an individual. Here also God could work in secret to transform that character by implanting new thoughts and feelings."[5] A heart that is first surrendered to God is the foundational mark of the birth of a true leader. A leader's purpose and vision are realized within the Potter's hands, and the giftings within the leader are released to serve not only God, but God's people. This leads to the last aspect of guidance.

A leader produces leaders.

Just as Paul describes in 1 Corinthians 12, the human body is a well-run, systematic flow of vital organs and body parts to ensure the body is functional, healthy, and does what is was intended to do. The lungs do not try to mimic or be like the kidneys, nor does the neck try to be the wrist. Each body part knows its own purpose and performs its own job. The church should function the same way. Christ is the head, and we are the body. God has provided leaders for the church, not for them to hand down orders, but for them to guide all those invested in the work of the church in this world and to help raise up the next generation of leaders. A leader helps people discover their own importance and their role within the building of the Kingdom. This unleashes new leaders and empowers them to serve God according to their own gifting and confidence.

Leadership Has a Destination

We have considered the ability and guidance aspects within our definition of leadership. Let's consider the third and final aspect of leadership: having a destination or desired goal.

I recall an opportunity my good friend and I had to tour around Soweto, which is located within Johannesburg, South Africa, with two students from

Texas, USA. Soweto is an urbanized township that has become a tourist attraction because of its rich history, rooted deep within the streets. As locals, we served as guides for the tour. However, in our youthful pride, neither of us would admit that we did not know our way around Soweto as well as it had been suggested we did. So, we did what any other person would do. My friend pulled out his smartphone and used Google Maps to guide us around the area. The overall tour was great and enlightening. Our guests really enjoyed every aspect of the tour — except when we gave late prompts and when we had them turn the wrong way down one-way routes. After the whole ordeal, I pondered on the situation. They rightfully trusted us because it was our "hometown advantage." We had visited each tourist attraction in Soweto multiple times since primary school and yet, with Uncle Google Maps by our side, we still failed to communicate the correct directions to them of where they needed to be. Why did this happen? We didn't have a known destination in mind or a thoughtful plan for how to get there.

If we were to be true guides or leaders, we needed to know and familiarize ourselves with the directions and destination in order for the trip to have gone as we desired. Leaders have this awesome opportunity as well. Leaders have the task of leading people to a desired goal or destination. When it comes to Kingdom leadership, the commonly highlighted destination is heaven. We often hear believers say, "Oh Pastor Jones, I can't wait until I get to heaven" or "Oh Mrs. Berry, I can't wait until the Lord comes." Don't get me wrong; seeing the Lord and experiencing our full redemption will be a great and wonderful moment! However, Jesus' life, ministry, and the whole of the Gospel makes such statements secondary to the task we've been given.

Biblical, Kingdom-minded servant leadership will always be based on two principles that God knows will change the world and create ripples throughout time: to love God with all our heart, mind and soul and to love our neighbor.

One moment where this difference is highlighted is recorded within the Gospel of Luke, chapter 24. This is the story of the two disciples' encounter with Jesus on the road to Emmaus. I encourage you to take a minute to look it up and read it. This refreshing passage is so revolutionary, and it gives us deeper insight into the very aspects we have been discussing: the ability of the leader, the guidance of the leader, and the destination of the leader. Just after a costly loss of their guide, our two companions in the text were distraught, disappointed, and hopeless after what they had witnessed in Jerusalem. A concealed Jesus was walking beside them and hearing them talk this out as an ordinary travel companion. It is possible that these two disciples had a livelihood or trade that they had left within moments of hearing Jesus teach. The miracles, the teachings, and the authority with which Jesus spoke transformed their understanding of God's plan for His people. They had believed their destination was to be citizens of a restored Israel with the Messiah, Jesus of Nazareth, reigning over all their enemies. Instead, their high hopes and expectations were met with the cruel fate of their Rabbi nailed and hung on a tree. No one could bring them out of this hopeless pit. No one except Jesus Himself, who was patiently hearing them out, rebuking their doubt, opening the Scriptures, visiting their home, and finally breaking bread before their eyes were opened.

Jesus expanded their perspective and understanding of what it meant to be a people of God in a broken world (BE). Jesus walked along the road and opened the Scriptures with them (DO). And their encounter with Jesus compelled them to get up and return to Jerusalem (GO). Our response to this same Gospel has been entrusted to each and every one of us. Our destination as a leader is our legacy. We are compelled to "go and make Christlike disciples of all the nations" in the power and authority He has given us. Our legacy is new believers entering into a heavenly Kingdom, a Kingdom here on Earth as it is in heaven, filled with Kingdom-principled people.

Leadership will forever be a popular topic in society. Experts will constantly revisit and reinvent principles in order to change and adapt to new cultural trends and global events. However, biblical, Kingdom-minded servant leadership will always be based on two principles that God knows will change the world and create ripples throughout time: to love God with all our heart, mind and soul and to love our neighbor. My brothers and sisters, this is the kind of leaders you and I are called to be.

CHAPTER 2

As You Begin: Knowing Why You Lead

Odily Díaz

Odily Díaz is the North Central Field Youth Coordinator and the Youth Ministry Academy Coordinator for Mesomerica, serving in San Salvador, El Salvador. Youth ministry is exciting to her because she gets to see God transform the lives of youth when they are given the opportunity to serve. Leadership development is an opportunity to put our gifts and talents to use in youth ministry.

Wesley's Fingerprint

Physical attacks. Travel dangers. Robberies. Murders. Social class disparities. Alcoholism. Prostitution. Street fights. These words name the difficult realities of many of our societies, but they are also descriptors of John Wesley's England.[1] Perhaps these opening words seem more like a list we would use to launch into a discussion on evangelism rather than one on leadership development. We would first ask, how do we help those engaged in these activities hear the Good News of the Gospel? John Wesley responded by preaching a revitalized and powerful message of holiness. His message, which had not been heard for a long time, was based on salvation, faith, holiness, and good works. Wesley's passionate preaching for social transformation brought in a great harvest — but why should this interest us in a book on leadership development? Because his work transitioned from a spontaneous revival to a movement which made history, thanks to its system of developing leaders.

As the movement grew, Wesley established a system of societies, classes, and bands. These provided mutual support for members, but they also served as a way to provide discipline to leaders who were not living up to what was expected of them as members of the society. The fast and unequaled growth of the Methodist societies in England generated a need for the laity to become involved in helping lead the movement. John Wesley established a system to organize classes in every city, delegating pastoral work to these passionate servants of the Lord.

Wesley himself was a pastor passionate for the work of the Lord, and he taught those lay leaders about pastoral ministry and biblical studies. As a rule, he would evaluate their work and character and provide them with a letter or card every three months which they could carry that would validate them as ministers. Wesley rediscovered the work, mission, love, compassion, commitment, and life of the first Christians. By dedicating his life in service to his God and Savior and then using this system, he met the needs of those whom Jesus himself came for: the needy.

Additionally, in this system Wesley showed a true interest in establishing a leadership platform to launch lay people into pastoral service. This discipleship process included the calling, preparation, and sending out of these laypeople, thus multiplying the number of servant leaders who could then respond to the great spiritual and social needs of the bands and classes.

This practice provided the church with a holistic system of development that did the following:

1. Provided a biblical form of pastoral care based on love

2. Developed committed lay leaders who loved and prayed for each other

3. Helped in holistic growth through the study of God's word

4. Strengthened the person's sense of belonging and communal life

5. Helped people be accountable to each other, fostering a life of transparency and social holiness.

In our strong history, we find the value of theological, social, and spiritual preparation. We do this through a process of teaching and learning where leaders are encouraged to pay close attention — both to leading others and to developing disciples to continue the work among youth and teens.

As we discuss leadership development, it is important to make sure we have several foundational principles in place. These principles are both for our own leadership practices and also to assist us in creating space and opportunities for our youth and teens to develop as leaders. We are going to look at the role of pastoral care, the importance of diverse voices, and the components that make up a supportive environment.

Through all of this, we must learn the importance of "teaching for real life," a phrase widely used in recent years. Studies show that successful education involves more than concepts; it also includes experiences and practices which serve to develop the students' abilities. Thus, it is imperative for a process to exist through which theoretical, technical, and practical knowledge is imparted to emerging leaders so they may be formed and sent out to serve the other youth of their society.

Pastoral Care

Félix Ortiz writes that pastoral care is "the work of the church in a particular place."[2] In other words, you and I must meet the needs of youth in our setting, community, and context. NYI is known for being as international as the many countries that form it, and this great adventure of ministry also turns into our responsibility. How does our particular place shape the work we are doing? How do the particular youth who make up our youth group shape the way we do the work of the church? If our youth ministry is not shaped by those who make up our youth group, it is a sign we are not taking the task of pastoral care very seriously. Before we can invest in youth and help them become leaders, we must know them well enough to see the gifts God has given them, even if they don't see them yet themselves.

We see Jesus as our great model in His pastoral work towards His disciples. Jesus constantly sought to help people grow. He counseled them, walked with them, served them, and was an inspiration to those who followed Him. He engaged in His pastoral work so faithfully because His calling was perfectly clear. Jesus did not say He was a good son, even though He was. He did not say He was a good leader or a good preacher, even though He was both of those things. He did not say He was a good doctor, even though He healed through miracles. He did not say He was a good teacher, even though His teaching was extraordinary. Isn't it interesting that when Jesus chose a description for Himself, He calls Himself a shepherd?!

> **Before we can invest in youth and help them become leaders, we must know them well enough to see the gifts God has given them, even if they don't see them yet themselves.**

> "I am the good shepherd; I know my sheep and my sheep know me—just as the Father knows me and I know the Father—and I lay down my life for the sheep. I have other sheep that are not of this sheep pen. I must bring them also. They too will listen to my voice, and there shall be one flock and one shepherd." (John 10:14-16, NIV)

This is especially meaningful in my language, Spanish, because we use the same word for shepherd and pastor. One of the most respectable professions is that of pastor, but many of us reject God's pastoral calling on our lives. All of us notice youth, both inside and outside, of our church who need someone to love, guide, teach, and encourage them. However, too often, we passively wait for someone else to take on the pastoral task. We have our own responsibilities and priorities and a hundred other reasons why we say no. But there is no reason that is good enough to reject such a calling from God.

Sometimes this calling is to vocational ministry; other times the call will look more like John Wesley's lay ministers. We all have a call to the work of pastoral care — to love and care for each other. "But you are a chosen people, a royal priesthood, a holy nation, God's special possession, that you may declare the praises of him who called you out of darkness into his wonderful light" (1 Peter 2:9).

Jesus is a model pastor for us because of how well He knew His sheep. Youth leaders and pastors know their youth very well and are looking for the right way to guide them. Still, we should always be transparent so that our disciples can know us as we truly are. Jesus gave His life for His sheep, and our teens and youth need people who are willing to make sacrifices for them as well.

Welcome Diverse Voices

Before we talk about the value of diversity, let's tackle the deceptively difficult word, "welcome." It is absolutely impossible to develop leaders if we hold tightly to all areas of our youth ministry. We must be willing to welcome others in and allow them to learn alongside us. While this is true for other adult leaders, it is especially true for our youth leaders.

The primary goal of developing a youth ministry is that youth may become spiritually mature. We desire for them to learn to live and think like Jesus. We want their faith to be seen in their attitudes, knowledge, and relationships with God, themselves, others, their community, and the world around them. The characteristics of a mature person in Christ are seen through the knowledge they attain, the convictions they internalize, and the behaviors they practice. If we focus on this premise, the youth in our ministries will reach a strong, fulfilling relationship with God, their leaders, and families. In turn, they will prosper in their personal lives. As we've discussed earlier, education of all sorts is at its best when it includes opportunities to put the lessons they are learning into practice. We must be welcoming and invite youth and other adults into leadership.

This will sometimes feel like a huge risk, but I think leaders need to take risks with some of the young people who are still in the process of growing and being formed. This should be done with supervision of course, always walking alongside them. We must create opportunities to develop others while on the way. I have heard some in the church say, "I had to work for it, so they should do the same." This is not welcoming. We should not be selfish. We need to help, promote, and empower young leaders to develop in every way possible. Let us not harbor fear in our hearts that young leaders will push us out or take our place! This is not healthy for anyone. It is also unfounded. We always need servant leaders in the church! Leadership is the primary resource in youth ministry. Through selfless leading and making space for others to lead, your life becomes your best educational tool. Who you are is the key factor in how you carry out the kind of discipleship youth need.

Learning what we don't know is best accomplished by welcoming diverse voices into our ministry.

Welcoming other leaders into ministry does more than just help them; it helps us as well. As in any other profession, it is necessary to attain a certain level of competency in your work. There is a particular level of knowledge, convictions, abilities, attitudes, and values that we must have in order to do the work of youth ministry well. The hardest part of any job is to know what we don't know. However, a youth leader must know what he/she needs to learn in order to grow as a leader.

Learning what we don't know is best accomplished by welcoming diverse voices into our ministry. Work with a team of people who have areas of knowledge and expertise different from yours so that you can have a wide spectrum of topics, thoughts, and ideas available to you to renew your ministry. Allow them to contribute their passion to the work being done.

Recognize the value of each member of your team and delegate responsibilities to each of them. Pray for those you want on your team who you believe have the abilities and talents you need. After a time of prayer and observation, invite them to work with you in the ministry. If you see that they are interested, prepare a plan to develop them or give them options for training so they can be efficient in their work. Open up. Reach out. Welcome in. Make space for new leaders to practice and learn.

As a final note for this section, it is no surprise that the more voices there are at the table, the more chance there is for disagreements. However, do not be afraid of conflict. Pray, and God will give you wisdom to face and redirect these conflicts toward the good. Work so that each member of the team embraces the vision and goals so that these can be achieved. Constantly evaluate the work to ensure you are going in the right direction. You will quickly begin to see the depth that comes to your ministry due to this diversity.

Creating a Supportive Environment

Once we've welcomed others onto our team, we need to make sure they will be challenged, feel safe trying new things, be able to give and receive feedback, and overall, be able to develop as a leader. As leaders committed to developing other leaders, we need to make sure the environment in which we are developing leaders is defined by the following eight traits.

Love

The main motivation for the youth leader should be love (John 13:34-35). This means loving your youth, no matter what they do. When youth feel loved and cared for, they typically respond in kind and emulate our witness. Everything we do that touches their lives is an investment, since they will embody and continue the example of their leaders by loving their neighbor as themselves. Love provides the foundation that will help you establish a meaningful friendship with your youth. This will allow them to feel safe when stepping out into leadership for the first time. Love will pave the way for them to believe you when you express confidence in their giftings. Try to engage their hearts so that they can trust you and see you not only as a leader, but as a friend who will be there when they need one.

Encouragement

Encouragement mobilizes youth to serve, and it is contagious. A youth leader must challenge youth to faithfully follow Christ but also encourage them to serve God with a thankful heart and respond to God's call on their lives. Work with them so that they can set out on this journey to develop as a leader and fulfill that calling. Tell them how much you appreciate their service to the church, their dedication and support, and encourage them to give more, providing new opportunities for service. This will make a difference in their lives.

Not long ago, one of our Youth Ministry Academy students in the region finished their studies and graduated with their diploma. He is an extrovert who likes to joke and have fun while also being professional. I had the privilege of teaching one of the courses that he took, and he told me he saw his lack of seriousness as a barrier to being in leadership and carrying out his pastoral calling. While we chatted, I tried to encourage him. A couple of weeks ago, he told me he was called by a church to be its pastor. He had believed that because of his character and temperament he would never be taken seriously, so it was a joy to hear the excitement in his voice! He is now serving the Lord as a pastor, teaching, caring for the flock and always recognizing God is forming him to care for others.

Character

According to D.L. Moody, "character is what you are in the dark."[3] God calls and raises youth leaders, using them for God's purposes. It is important for them to know that we cannot give others something we do not first possess. Ignoring the question of character is to abandon the foundation of our ministry. This is why God spends so much time preparing His servants. It took God 13 years to prepare Joseph to be the second-in-command over all of Egypt. God invested 80 years preparing Moses to lead Israel out of Egypt and three years preparing Saul of Tarsus in post-graduate work in Arabia before sending him out as an apostle. God will form us all along our journey. Sometimes the places we find ourselves do not seem like they could have anything to do with ministry, nor could they be used by God for any good purpose. However, God can use any experience or circumstance to shape our character if we release it to Him for His purposes. So, encourage young leaders to be patient in the process of having their character formed.

Without character, ministry simply becomes a religious activity, or even worse, religious "business." Pharisees called what they were doing "ministry," but Jesus called it "hypocrisy." He knew they were more worried about their own reputation than about their character, and they were more interested in receiving praises from others than God's approval.[4]

Integrity

Similar to character is integrity. The word integrity comes from the same Latin root as the word "whole" and encompasses the whole person. Just as we talk about whole numbers, we can also talk about a person who is whole, not divided. A person of integrity lives rightly and doesn't act differently depending on the circumstances. A person of integrity acts the same way in private and in public. In the Sermon on the Mount, Jesus talked about people of integrity as being those who were "pure of heart" (Matthew 5:8).

Hold all leaders, adult leaders and youth leaders, to a high standard of integrity. Provide space for accountability to emphasize the importance of being the same in private and in public. This kind of discipline will also help shape young leaders so that accountability becomes an expected part of leadership for them.

Respect

In order for us to help develop a youth as a leader, they must respect us. If youth are going to respect us, they must know that we respect them. Be willing to listen to our youth without talking. Let them know they are important to us. Be interested in the things they are interested in. Listen to and take seriously their ideas and opinions. Listening to them closely produces in youth and teens the desire to communicate with us, and it helps to foster an environment of respect.

Invest

Your adult and youth leaders are giving of themselves and their time to serve and to grow as leaders. Learn to invest in them. You do not need to be a millionaire to do this — you will be surprised to learn how far training, mentoring, or a coaching session can take you. While much will be gained through the practical experience of leadership opportunities, more formal times of mentoring and training will have a significant impact on your leaders.

Service

Christian leaders must be servant leaders. A youth leader must lead through their example and learn to serve as Jesus served. Jesus said, "the Son of Man came not to be served but to serve" (Matthew 20:28). This means that we should worry not so much for our needs but for the needs of others; we should not demand other people's time but give ours away, and all of this without expecting recognition.

Gratitude

While we don't lead expecting recognition, we should be quick to express our gratitude to those who are leading with us. Always thank them for their service. Recognize their achievements. Give them feedback in private. One of my professors in a leadership course pointed out that we tend to always begin with something they are doing well, after which we insert the famous, "but...." For example, "Carlos, you played very well Sunday. I wanted to congratulate you for your impeccable playing, *but* please do not wear those pants again. Remember you are leading youth and your 'witness' is important." No one in their right mind would accept this kind of conditional compliment. You should either congratulate or call out, not try to do both to "soften" the blow. We must acknowledge and be honest with our team in such a way that no one is offended because they know you are doing it for their good and the good of the team.

Philosophy of Pastoral Leadership

Now that we have covered these foundational elements for leadership development, it is imperative that you establish your philosophy of pastoral leadership. A philosophy of pastoral leadership allows you to describe the basic values which you will use in order to build your youth leader development model. It should reflect what you consider to be important, such as:

- a theological perspective for youth leadership
- a vision of being and reality
- a vision of knowledge
- a theological and philosophical vision of people
- a vision of learning and the nature of teaching
- the role of leadership
- the role or place of the youth leaders in the overall ministry of the church

In summary, a philosophy of pastoral leadership will answer the questions "Why do you need a youth ministry?" and "What guides your youth leadership development strategies?" This philosophy of pastoral leadership changes depending on the context, the vision, the formation of the leader, and the size of the congregation. Additional elements will arise out of specific social contexts.

Conclusion

As you continue in this book, you will be challenged in ever-expanding circles of leadership development, starting with self-leadership. "One of the tensions any leader must face is balancing leading others and leading oneself. In fact, many leadership experts question a person's ability to lead others and guide people when they do not have the capacity to practice self-leadership in their lives and personal goals."[5]

When we are leading others, people will not always remember what we said at different workshops or talks, but they will remember if we are disorganized and unprepared. The previous quote calls us to reflect on our ability to lead ourselves. Are we disciplined? Do we set and work toward personal goals? As leaders, we must always strive to lead our lives rightly, exert self-control, know how to manage our agendas, and have a good understanding of why we do what we do.

With these disciplines in place, we can keep our focus on the call of God on our lives to serve teens and youth. If we stray from this path, we will either fail or build a kingdom of no consequence because God will not be present. Romans 11:29 states, "for God's gifts and his call are irrevocable." We cannot deny, God is the force that moves and pushes us to accomplish our objective, which is to seek the transformation of the lives which God has entrusted to us.

A long-term ministry is achieved through self-leadership, which allows us to know what is important; first in our personal lives, but also in our families, the ministry, and all areas of life. For a ministry to be successful and consistent, it is necessary to build good relationships. There is no better program or activity to invest in than your leadership team, communicating with them and trusting in them. Do not use fear to gain authority; well-earned authority will reward everyone involved.

The following chapters will also challenge us in how we work with all leaders in the church. A healthy youth ministry involves your pastor and church leaders. This is a big challenge, but some of our projects include the whole congregation. It is indispensable to have credibility and trust among youth leaders and the rest of your leaders. Be creative and invite them to get to know your projects. I encourage you to take the initiative. It has been shown that church leaders want to have good relationships with youth leaders, but often times they do not know where to begin.

A powerful tool in the process of developing healthy relationships with these other leaders is service. Start by discovering ways you can come alongside and support what they are doing. Maintain a meaningful relationship with your leaders. It is important to have good lines of communication with your pastor, colleagues, and leaders of your congregation. Learn to see them as a resource for your own ministry.

The goal for all these leadership principles is ultimately to help us be more faithful in engaging our youth in leadership development. Being a leader is not doing the work of others. If you remember Moses before he received Jethro's advice (Exodus 18:14), Moses was doing everything for everybody. Moses was serving the people, but being a leader is working with others to help them learn how to do something themselves. This is what Moses did after following Jethro's advice (Exodus 18:21-22) and what Jesus did when He sent out the Twelve and later the seventy.

Jesus didn't do ministry to and for His disciples; He invited them in and did ministry with them.

All through Scripture, we see how God raised up leaders to accomplish God's purposes. We also see how Jesus invested time in forming and educating the leaders He gathered around Himself. Jesus came to reconcile humanity with God, but He also chose and formed leaders to carry out this work of bringing God's love and reconciliation to the world. Jesus knew He would return to the Father and that these leaders were being prepared for the task of moving the early church forward.

Jesus' model is our model. Jesus didn't do ministry to and for His disciples; He invited them in and did ministry with them. Applying this model to our ministry contexts, we need to make sure we are inviting teens and youth in and doing ministry with them, rather than to or for them. Jesus always used leaders to accomplish His work, and if we want to follow His example, it is time for us to stop doing things by ourselves. Instead, we need to invest time into identifying and training leaders.

God wants us to use the leadership model Jesus gave us. He longs for us to get rid of our guises, appearances, and masks. You do not need to pretend to be someone else — Jesus' blood, grace, forgiveness, love, and power are all you need. Teens and youth need leaders willing to open up their lives, homes, and hearts. They need men and women — adults and young adults — willing to show their scars in order to heal others, willing to be open in love so that other souls are saved, willing to become vulnerable and give their lives for others.

Youth are the first of our values as NYI. They are important and needed to continue on with the work our Lord Jesus Christ gave us. Recently, I heard a friend say something I liked very much; "We are educating and empowering the generation that will educate and empower our children." I think she is right! It is up to us to do a good job for the future of the church and the world.

CHAPTER 3

Self-Leadership:
Investing in Our Own Development as Leaders

Kat Wood

Kat Wood serves as a co-pastor in Greater Manchester, United Kingdom. Youth ministry is exciting for her because she loves seeing young people engage with God. Kat believes good leaders should be looking to help shape, grow, and empower the next generation of leaders so they can serve the Church in a way that is true to who they are in Christ.

Before we get started, I want to share a bit about myself. My husband Joseph and I have two children, Evelyn who is 5 and Miriam who is almost 2, and a slightly insane dog named Dixie. I grew up in the church. I attended a Baptist church with my parents until I was 2 years old, and we moved to a different town about an hour away. It was here that my parents first discovered the Church of the Nazarene. There was no local Baptist church, so after checking with their previous pastor to make sure the Nazarenes weren't "some kind of weird cult," they started attending the Church of the Nazarene at the bottom of the hill from where we lived. We have been members ever since.

When I was around 16 years old, I decided church was not relevant to me. I decided I could believe in Jesus and God and still do all the things I wanted to do — the things my friends were doing — and church did not need to be a part of my life. I convinced myself that the Bible was outdated and that all the do's and do-not's no longer mattered. All I needed was to believe in God and believe that Jesus died for me. The reality was that I did not want to surrender myself, my life, my all to God, so I spent the next four years living life my way — which mainly involved sex, drugs, rock 'n' roll — and no commitment to anything "Christian."

After four years of going my own way, I finally surrendered and allowed God to break into my life. I realized that it should mean something to say I believe in God, to accept His love for me, and to accept Jesus, His Son, dying for me. I knew I had to start taking what I believed seriously. I had to allow my beliefs to shape me, because when you have a genuine encounter with Christ, your life should no longer look the same. I started attending church again and was intentional about getting involved in its life and ministry. Over the next 12 months, I heard, understood, and eventually gave in to God's call on my life to become a pastor. I signed up for the Bachelor of Arts in theology and pastoral studies at Nazarene Theological College in Manchester, UK (NTC), and the rest is history.

One of the key truths of leadership is the importance of self-leadership. If we are going to lead others well, we need to be people of character, find ways to invest in ourselves, know who we are in God, and find times to intentionally pause and reflect on our leadership. Thus, finding ways to better engage youth in leadership development doesn't start with them; it starts with us.

What follows in this chapter is some of what I have learned about self-leadership during my time in the ministry. I hope it helps you as you explore what it means to be in leadership and to develop the emerging leaders around you.

Integrity

Character matters.

As a part of my training to become a pastor at NTC, I was on placement (internship) at the Church of the Nazarene in Longsight, Manchester. I was a placement student there for three and a half years. During my second year, one of my responsibilities was to visit a lady who was housebound and could rarely make it to church gatherings. One week when I had my regular meeting with my line-manager, she asked me if I had been to see this lady. I told her I had been trying to get through to her on the phone to arrange a visit, but I never got through to talk to her, so I had sent a card and that I would try again next week. The reality was, I had phoned once and after letting it ring four or five times I hung up. I kept meaning to phone again, but I hadn't. I kept meaning to go around to her flat, but I hadn't. I kept meaning to send a card, but I hadn't. When I got in that evening I wrote a card and sent it the next morning in case my line-manager would check up on me and find out that I had never sent one. Even then, the purpose behind me sending a card was not the care of the lady I was meant to be visiting but to protect my own back.

It was this incident that made me realise that I had an integrity problem — I was not an honest person. I would tell myself it was not really a big deal: I was not lying maliciously to get people in trouble or spreading vicious rumours; I would only tell "little" lies or not tell the whole truth if it meant I would not get in trouble or if it would protect my reputation. This really shook me. Here I was training to be a pastor and yet I was not a person who could be trusted to tell the truth. Since then, I have made sure I am honest with people. When I forget something, instead of making up an excuse, I say I am sorry. If I have not fulfilled a responsibility of some kind, instead of only telling part of the truth so I don't look bad, I apologise, take full responsibility for not following through, and then try to resolve it. Integrity, your character, is really important when it comes to leadership.

In our Leadership Development Initiative, we use a series of books by Tim Elmore called *Habitudes*[1] as the focus of the mentoring relationships that form the core part of the development of new leaders. These books use a series of images to teach good leadership habits and attitudes. The first image in

A person's character will influence the decisions they make, the way they see others, and the way they lead.

the first book is an iceberg. Elmore uses the imagery of an iceberg because 90% of the iceberg is below the water. He writes, "The iceberg represents your leadership. The 10% above the water is your skill. The 90% below the water is your character. It's what's below the surface that sinks the ship."[2] I think all of us could think of at least one leader — politician, pastor, athlete, or celebrity — who has been caught up in fraud, extramarital affairs, cheating, drugs, embezzling, or just not being a very nice person. It was not their skills that led them to make those decisions but their character.

Our character as leaders is important. A person's character will influence the decisions they make, the way they see others, and the way they lead. It is very important for us to take time to work on our character.

Here are two things that have helped me to develop, grow, and protect my character:

The first is to regularly spend time praying and reading Scripture. Our desire as Christians is to be Christlike. Therefore, as Christian leaders, our desire should be to lead like Christ. If we want to be Christlike leaders, we need to know who Christ is, and He is revealed to us through the Scriptures and the Holy Spirit. We also need to regularly make time to allow God to search us and shape us as we both listen and speak to Him through prayer. This will look different for everyone. Not all of you will pray or absorb Scripture in the same way. Some of you will be great readers; others will prefer to listen to a podcast or watch a sermon or lecture on YouTube. Some of you will enjoy solitary reflection whilst others of you learn better when discussing ideas with others. There are others who love to process and express themselves through art. My point is, how you do this it is not as important as the fact that you do it.

The second is to have people around you who have permission to speak truth into your life and, more importantly, who you make time to see and listen to as well. These are the people who will help you work on your character flaws and celebrate your character strengths.

Invest

Investing in ourselves enables us to invest better in others.

Bertha has a bank account with a good amount of money in it. It is in a healthy place. Sometimes she makes withdrawals several times a day and at other times only a couple of times a week. There are circumstances which result in Bertha making large withdrawals and small withdrawals for others. Sooner or later, the money in Bertha's account dwindles until she has next to nothing left. Bertha notices this, but she simply does not have the time to get to the bank and make a deposit. One day Bertha notices the account is empty. She keeps meaning to make the time to get down to the bank, but things keep popping up and so she spends time on them instead of making a deposit into her account. The need to make withdrawals, however, does not stop and before she knows it her account is not just empty but it is overdrawn. Bertha's account is now in an unhealthy place. She finally takes the time to go to the bank and make a deposit because she knows she needs to get back into the positive. However, she is so deeply in debt that it is a real struggle to get her account back from the negative into the positive.

It can be easy for those in leadership to be like Bertha. We can be so caught up in focusing on what we are trying to achieve — the ministries that we lead, the tasks before us, the people we are leading and caring for and the responsibilities we have — that we rarely spend any time focusing on ourselves. Before we know it, we are so invested in our ministry and the lives of those around us that we have forgotten to invest in ourselves. When we make too many withdrawals without enough deposits, we end up in an unhealthy place. How can we invest in developing those around us when we have nothing left to give?

I know that for me to function at my best, I need to make time and space for myself. I am an introvert who loves being around people, but I know I need time on my own in order to recharge my batteries and feel refreshed. In my experience, this is not something leadership lends itself to naturally. It is more common for leaders to be expected to be "doing" all the time if they are to be effective. It took me a while to learn this about myself, but I now know that in order for me to be effective, I have to make time to simply "be," rather than constantly "do."

In July 2016, I returned to work after having 10 months off for maternity leave with my second child. I was excited to be back at work in the church because I had missed it. I love my job and all the opportunities and challenges it brings. As I was happy to be back, I threw myself back into my role, but this time it was harder. I found it a lot more difficult being a mum of two than being a mum of one. I found it harder to get the right balance between work and home and friends and family and hobbies and just life. I found myself giving in so many areas, but I wasn't finding the time to invest in myself. Thus, I began to struggle a little bit. I just felt emotionally, physically, and spiritually drained. I knew I had to do something about this, so in November 2016 I booked myself on to a four-day silent retreat at a monastery. It was exactly what I needed. Each morning one of the monks would speak to the group (there were about 15 of us) and give us something to reflect on for that day. I would join the monks for meals and worship four times a day and the rest of the time I spent reading, praying, walking, sleeping, thinking, and

Finding ways for you to receive as well as give will mean you have more to give to others and you will be able to do so from a much healthier place.

sometimes just sitting. There is something quite unique about spending time in silence and the only words you hear (besides the occasional "pass the butter") are words of worship and Scripture — both read and sung. For me, taking this time and space to invest in myself was life-giving, and I came back refreshed. I had experienced a time of blessing, and I came back ready to pour that blessing into the lives of those I met. This is something I now plan to do yearly.

I am not suggesting we all go on a silent retreat, as this would be heaven for some, and for others it would be a nightmare. Nonetheless, carving out time and space for resting in God's presence, however you do that, is an important thing to do. Finding ways for you to receive as well as give will mean you have more to give to others, and you will be able to do so from a much healthier place.

What gives you joy in life? I really like going to the cinema. Watching films and entering into other people's stories makes me happy. So I make sure I get to go as often as I can, even if it means saying no to a meeting or making my admin wait one more day. It is important for us to find out what it is that brings us joy, whatever that might be — dance, family, friends, sport, crafts, poetry, walking, art, watching funny cat videos on the internet, traveling — and then make the time to do it. This will help sustain your wellbeing in leadership and enable you to invest in others from a healthy place.

We also need to make time to invest in our own development as leaders. Education and teaching, whether it is in a formal or informal setting, is important when developing leaders. I believe, as leaders, we should be continually developing, even when we are developing others. Attending conferences, reading books, going to seminars, taking relevant courses, discussing ideas — these will help to shape, stretch, challenge, encourage, and move you forward as leaders. If we want to develop leaders, we must also be developing ourselves as leaders.

May we not be like Bertha. Remember to make deposits as well as withdrawals.

Identity

Knowing who we are in God enables growth.

Identity is an important issue for me because it is something I have wrestled with for many years now. I was bullied for most of my teenage years. I often felt like I didn't quite fit in. I always had friends that were a part of the "popular" crowd, but they wouldn't want to hang out with me in public; I was never cool enough. I can still remember the day I showed up to the evening service at our church, and there was a big pile of sleeping bags and pillows in the foyer. It turns out one of the girls in the church had invited all the girls at church for a sleepover at her house — everyone except me. Ouch! This had a huge impact on my self-esteem during some very formative years of my life. As a result, I would seek out my worth in other people and possessions. I was defined by my relationships and by the things I had. It took me several years to fully accept and understand what it really meant to be known and loved by God. Having my identity found and rooted in who I am in God — seen, known, loved, called, set-apart, precious, unique, forgiven, gifted, mission-partner, empowered by the Holy Spirit, a child of God — has given me a security in my identity that has helped shape my leadership and my ministry.

Knowing ourselves, our strengths and our weaknesses, is really helpful when it comes to leadership and developing the leaders around us because it can help us identify why we react, respond, or function in a certain way. When I was first asked if I would be a part of this writing project for Global NYI, my initial reaction was one of self-doubt: "I'm not the right person; who would want to listen to what I have to say about leadership?" As I said before, I have wrestled with the issues of identity and self-esteem for a long time, and although I am much, much better than I used to be, those negative thoughts still creep in from time to time. One of my weaknesses is that I am very self-critical. However, since I am aware of this, I can usually spot when it is happening, address it, and re-think how I should respond to the situation. So, when I recognized the self-doubt creeping in, I took a minute and began to think about my experience of leadership over the last 12 years.

My list quickly grew and included leadership roles such as youth camp coordinator and spiritual coordinator for the district youth camp, vice president of the district NYI council, vice president of the district NMI council, associate pastor, and co-pastor. I began to remember my experiences in starting ministries, closing ministries, a church plant, and various forms of outreach into different communities. I remembered that I am on the district Board of Ministry and that I oversee the Leadership Development Initiative for our district. I don't say any of this to brag or to make myself sound important, but rather to point out how my self-doubt was not based in the reality of my life experiences. I do have something to say on the issue of leadership and leadership development after all. The next time you find yourself doubting your abilities to take on a certain task or lead a particular ministry, I invite you to go through a similar process. Be honest with yourself, and make a list of the experiences you have had; recognize how God used those experiences to prepare you for the next opportunity ahead.

Knowing your strengths and weaknesses is also useful because it helps you make sure you have the right team around you. There is a well known parable about a group of blind men being introduced to an elephant for the first time. As they reach out and touch the elephant, each one comes up with a different description of what the elephant looks like.

If everyone on your team is stood at the front of the elephant, then an elephant is likely to only ever be a spear or a snake.

If everyone on your team is stood at the back of the elephant, then an elephant is likely to only ever be a rope (that sometimes gets a little smelly!).

Likewise, if everyone on your team is detail orientated, then it is likely that you will lose sight of the bigger picture. On the other hand, if everyone on your team is a big-picture thinker, then it is likely that the big picture will never be fully realised as the details of what needs to be done in order to accomplish the big picture get lost. The truth is, God created us and gifted us differently, and we need each other. Paul uses that great imagery of the Church as the body of Christ, and all the parts are important and needed in order for the body to function as it was created to.

In January 2017, my role at Ashton Church of the Nazarene changed from associate pastor to co-pastor. A big part of this transition was for me and my co-pastor, Carl, to sit down and look at our strengths and our weaknesses. We looked at where our gifts lay, and in light of that decided how the different responsibilities of leading the church should be split between us. Carl's giftings are particularly strong in the areas of vision, strategic thinking, and teaching. My giftings are particularly strong in the areas of relational ministry, pastoral care, and getting alongside those on the margins. This does not mean we do not speak into what the other is doing and what they're responsible for. We are a team, and we work best when we work together, but our main responsibilities lie in the areas we are strongest. Everyone has strengths. Everyone has weaknesses. We are strongest and can achieve the best results when we identify our weaknesses and work together in a way that compliments one another's gifts. Otherwise, we might end up with all smelly tails and no trunk.

We need to make sure it is God setting our priorities and not the expectations of others.

Knowing ourselves also protects us from projection. In leadership, it can be easy for us to feel the weight of other people's expectations when they are projected onto us. I have known several developing leaders who have allowed the expectation of others, either true or imagined, prevent them from becoming the leader they were called to be. To try and meet the expectations of tens or hundreds of people is exhausting. This is not to say we will not have responsibilities we need to fill as leaders. Instead, we need to make sure it is God setting our priorities and not the expectations of others. To constantly compare ourselves to this leader or that leader prevents us from becoming the leader we are called to be. God called you and gifted you for leadership because of who you are. Trust that He knows what He is doing. We still need to learn and grow and be shaped as we develop in leadership, but we need to make sure it is God doing the shaping and not us trying to force ourselves to look like someone we are not.

It can also be easy for us to project ourselves onto young leaders we are seeking to develop. It is tempting, when looking for those who we are going to develop as leaders, to seek out people who are like us. After all, we are leaders, and if they are like us, think like us, and have the same gifts as us, then they will be a good leader too. This may well be the case, but I also wonder how many potential leaders are overlooked because they did not meet our idea of what a leader is. There are numerous times in the story of God where He chose people no one expected to be chosen and they did great things in, with, and through God. As we look for potential new leaders to develop, it is important that we do not simply project ourselves on to them, but instead allow the Holy Spirit to guide us in how to help them develop. God might want to surprise you beyond anything you can hope or imagine.

The journey of finding out who we are in God is a journey worth going on, because all too often we allow the world to shape our picture of ourselves rather than our loving, merciful, and gracious God. Identity will impact your leadership whether you want it to or not. The truth is, all that we do flows out of who we are. Knowing who we are, having our identity rooted in God, and understanding our strengths and our weaknesses will help us understand our leadership and how we look for and develop the leaders around us.

Insight

Pause and reflect.

This may sound simple and obvious, but it needs to be said: it is important to take the time to think about the who, what, where, when, why, and how of what we are doing as leaders. Again, it seems obvious. Of course we need to think about what we are doing! However, in the busy life of a leader, creating space to pause and reflect on what is happening often gets pushed to the side. Continuing to move forward and "produce" often gains priority over re-flecting. If we want to be intentional in what we are doing, if we want people and ministries to develop, if we want to see things change, then we need to make the time to ask these questions.

Our leaders and those we lead tend to ask us what we are doing, what our next big event is, or what have we accomplished recently. Very few people will ask us if we have spent time reflecting on the culture being formed in our ministry or if we have identified the cause of the subtle change in the attitude of our volunteers. Without taking time for intentional reflection, small problems or minor shifts away from our mission eventually become major issues before they are attended to. We need to talk to our leaders, find ways to be accountable for times of reflection, and take the time to do it.

Conclusion

Leadership is a rewarding, challenging, frustrating, stretching, encouraging, equipping, fulfilling, and awesome responsibility within the Church. Whether you are new to leadership or you are an experienced leader looking to develop the emerging leaders around you, remember:

1. **Integrity.** Character matters. Spend as much time developing what is beneath the surface as you do the gifts and talents that are most evident; it was what was beneath the surface that sank the Titanic.

2. **Invest.** Investing in yourself enables you to better invest in others. Self-care is an important part of leadership, and it is important to model to those leaders we are developing. Don't be like Bertha; make deposits as well as withdrawals.

3. **Identity.** Knowing who you are in God enables growth. Knowing ourselves — our strengths and our weaknesses — and having our identity rooted in God enables us to grow in to the leaders God intended us to be and to help us get the right team around us.

4. **Insight.** Pause and reflect. If we want our people and ministries to grow and develop, then making time in the busyness of leadership to pause and reflect on the who, what, where, why, and how of what we are doing is essential.

May the Peace of Christ, which surpasses all understanding, be with you as you seek to follow Him, and as you lead and develop leaders within His Church.

CHAPTER 4

Followers to Leaders:
Awakening in Youth the Call to Lead

Thiago Nieman Ambrósio

Thiago Nieman Ambrósio serves as the executive secretary of NYI Brazil and as the District President of NYI Minas Gerais in Belo Horizonte, Minas Gerais. Thiago sees youth ministry as the most dynamic and attractional ministry of the church. Leadership development is important for Thiago because he believes today's leaders have to be committed to forming tomorrow's leaders.

Have you ever been witness to something I call the "imposition of a leader"? I have lived through this in many churches. The imposition of a leader, who is not a leader, is a misguided approach to identifying a leader, often for the youth ministry of the church. This problematic approach begins by observing all of the youth and looking for the one who "looks" like a leader. The first question you are trying to answer is, who is the most talkative? For a person to be a leader, he or she needs to communicate well with everyone. As you continue to observe, the second question you need to answer is, who is doing the most? A good leader has to know how to work hard. In the "imposition of a leader" approach, these are often the only two points being considered for a new leader to be chosen. The selected youth is then called forward and introduced to the youth group as their new "leader." The worst scenarios are when the new "leader" is not even consulted at any point to see if he or she is willing to take on the many responsibilities of youth ministry.

This is probably the worst approach we can take to find a leader, and yet God in His infinite mercy and love can transform even these misguided efforts and bring success to a situation that seems bound to fail. Even when God transforms a situation like this, it is still likely that this young youth leader has had to survive a lot of unnecessary fear and frustration. The act of being imposed as the leader usually means that they have carried the burden of leadership without any support system around them to help them learn and grow. In the best situations, they survive and figure out a strategy out on their own. In the worst situations, our actions scar a young leader from future service in the church.

Friends, there is a better way. In this chapter, we will discuss how we can help youth move from followers to leaders. We will talk about how we can help awaken the call of leadership in youth and what our responsibility is towards these young leaders.

Awaken the Call

How do we help awaken the call of leadership in young leaders? First, we must be in constant prayer for our youth. Youth are going through a dynamic process of learning who they are, what they like, what matters to them, and so much more. Even more challenging, what they think about who they are, what they like, and what matters to them can change daily. As we begin to invite our youth to see themselves as leaders and to take on leadership roles, we must be prayerfully seeking the wisdom of the Holy Spirit. We must try to identify what ways the Holy Spirit is already at work in their hearts. Despite their insecurities and changing beliefs about themselves, we must help them imagine what is God calling them to. This process of awakening the call of leadership in youth is primarily about helping them become the person God created and gifted them to be and not so much about filling empty positions in the church's ministry. God has gifted the church with all that we need to do the work we are called to. Sometimes we will be able to see giftings in our youth that they do not yet see in themselves. Encouraging them to try something new is significantly different than forcing them to take on a role just because someone needs to do it, and yet this can look similar from the outside. This is why we need to be praying for our youth and seeking the guidance of the Holy Spirit through this whole process.

> If young people never see someone leading who represents their ethnicity or gender, their age or their abilities, or someone from a background similar to their own, then we send the message that those differences disqualify them from leadership.

The second key element in awakening the call of leadership in youth is to be intentional about whom they see in leadership roles and whom they see preaching in the church. If young people never see someone leading who represents their ethnicity or gender, their age or their abilities, or some-one from a background similar to their own, then we send the message that those differences disqualify them from leadership. We would never make such a statement; however, it is exactly what we are unintentionally proclaiming when we don't find ways to honor the diversity of the Body of Christ in visible and meaningful ways.

With these two foundational elements, we can begin to talk with youth about their interests, passions, and giftings and how those can be given back to God for God to use. This is not the simplest task; it takes time. But the truth is that not all leaders can be identified by picking out the people who talk the most, show up the most, and work the most as we mentioned in the beginning of this chapter. It is also important to remember that someone who doesn't seem ready to lead right now might still be a great leader someday. They might just need some more time. The best way to identify leaders and potential leaders is to discern if their life reflects the values of Christ, and then, as we consider the variety of situations a leader might find himself or herself in, we can begin to identify behaviors which would indicate a readiness for leadership. This may include:

- An unsolicited desire to support the work of the church. Even without having a specific role, a leader will be the kind of person who sees what needs to be done and will offer to help. This definitely includes work done behind the scenes. A true leader doesn't need recognition in order to serve.
- An ability to bring out the best in people. The strongest leaders do not work alone, but they bring others along with them on the journey.
- An openness to feedback. Leaders know how to listen and respect their parents, mentors, and leaders.
- A passion for souls. A Christian leader should carry the awareness of our purpose as the church to share the great love of the Lord with each person we interact with.
- Adaptability. All ministry, but especially youth ministry, requires the ability to respond in helpful ways to unexpected changes in our plans. A leader adapts to these changes and works creatively to find solutions.

These characteristics of a good leader are not always easy to identify. Some characteristics will be obvious on their own; others will be hard to see until we begin to give our youth some more responsibility and observe how they respond. Sometimes we'll need to pay extra attention to see if some of these qualities are present in a rather "raw" or "undeveloped" form. Either way, the best way to help our youth see their own leadership potential and to help develop that potential is to motivate them and give them room to grow. Give them a chance to develop their skills more and more, let them innovate, and provide them with the autonomy to show what they can really do. This transitions us into the mentoring stage of developing young leaders.

Mentoring

Mentoring is simply the act of someone with a significant amount of experience sharing their knowledge and skill with a new leader. It is essential in the life of a young leader, and youth can greatly benefit from having one or even multiple mentors. The work of a mentor is to help their mentee begin to see the work they have been tasked with from new perspectives. The mentor comes alongside and shares their observations, draws attention to areas of concern, and asks thought-provoking questions to help the young leader think more broadly about their task. The focus is not to critique or make decisions for the mentee, but to share insights from the mentor's own life experiences in order to help the mentee learn along the way. When done well, mentorship will often reflect the tone of a trusted friendship or sacred fellowship.

Today I am much more aware of the need to mentor young leaders. The first time I was asked to lead, I was about 15 years old. We were a group of five teenagers between 15 and 18 years old. An entire generation had moved on from the youth group, and leadership had not been prepared for the future. We found ourselves faced with the questions I shared at the beginning of this chapter. Who, out of these five youth, is the most communicative and who knows how to work a little bit in the church? By the mercy of God, among the five of us, each one had a characteristic we needed in leadership, and what began to happen was that we found a way for all of us to work together.

When done well, mentorship will often reflect the tone of a trusted friendship or sacred fellowship. We had no knowledge of leadership or the significance of the opportunity we had been given, but something came into our hearts that made us want to give our best. We had no mentors or guides; it was only through the mercy and empowerment of the Lord and the love for teens and youth that the Lord started to nurture dreams and plans in our hearts.

One of the first decisions we had to make was when to have the youth service. It had previously been held on Sundays in the middle of the afternoon. We thought a better option would be to change the service to Saturday. Many were against it, but it was the best change we made as we had great results on Saturdays. We also faced the challenge of who would preach. We didn't know how to preach; we didn't feel well versed in the Bible, but God was guiding and using us, and the fruits of our faithfulness to God began to show as teenagers and youth began to give themselves to the love of Christ and to the work of the church.

I can look back on that time and see how we developed ourselves, but the journey was long and the path was hard because we did not have much guidance or support. It was not easy, but I believe in the higher purpose of Christ for our journeys as we all became leaders who sought to develop other leaders. We became the mentors we did not have.

The reality is that many adults do not have or have struggled to find mentors. It seems that one of the most common reasons given for not wanting to mentor someone else is the insecurity people feel from not having been mentored themselves. Unfortunately, this kind of response only pushes the problem onto the next generation. If we have not been mentored ourselves, we should continue seeking out that type of relationship. Nonetheless, as we turn to Scripture, there are a number of insights we can gather from the mentor/mentee relationships we find there:

The relationship matters. In Paul's first letter to Timothy, we quickly see how deeply Paul cared for Timothy as he addresses his letter, "To Timothy my true son in the faith." (1 Timothy 1:2). In eight of Paul's letters to various churches and individuals, he mentions Timothy in some way, highlighting the fact that Paul saw Timothy as more than just a co-worker, but also as a part of his family. The mentoring relationship is not a transactional arrangement where the mentee will have some new facts and excellent tips shared with them if they show up. In mentoring, the relationship matters. As we build trust, this will be a time when our mentee will share their struggles and fears, and we need to acknowledge those emotions and help them find a way to move past those barriers. This will often happen as we share our own stories of struggle and growth. In the end, you have to be willing to open up and invest in the relationship, not just the person.

The journey matters. All four of the gospel accounts contain stories of Jesus' day-to-day life with His disciples. While this is viewed as discipleship, rightly so, Jesus was also forming the individuals who would become the leaders of the church. Jesus didn't just gather the disciples together once a week or twice a month for a leadership class. He walked with them daily and allowed them to see how He treated people, how He responded to their needs, how He taught about God, and how He loved even the outsider. This faithful journeying together cannot be replaced by a simpler, short-cut method. The journey shapes and forms us, as well as those we are mentoring. We will talk more about this at the end of the chapter.

Our affirmation matters. Scripture tells us that Joshua had served as Moses' aide since his youth. Moses had given Joshua different key responsibilities over the years. Joshua even went part of the way up Mount Sinai with Moses when Moses met with God. However, one of the most powerful lessons we can learn from Moses in the way he mentored Joshua was his public affirmation of Joshua's leadership. In Deuteronomy 31:7, Moses announces Joshua as his successor: "Then Moses summoned Joshua and said to him in the presence of all Israel, 'Be strong and courageous, for you must go with this people into the land that the Lord swore to their ancestors to give them, and you must divide it among them as their inheritance'" (emphasis added). When our mentee steps out to lead, we should affirm their leadership. This is not only significant for our mentee, but just as Moses affirmed Joshua "in the presence of all Israel," those our mentee will be serving will benefit greatly from hearing your voice affirming the leadership skills you see in their new leader.

As we conclude this section on mentoring, it is important to note the responsibility faced by the person being mentored. They are accountable for following-through on responsibilities given to them, for showing up to scheduled meetings with their mentor, to show respect to their mentor, and overall, to be engaged in the mentoring process. Set mutual expectations at the beginning of the process so both of you know what to expect and what you want to get out of your time together.

Trainings

Once we have developed the mentoring relationship, another way we can invest in young leaders is to offer times of more formalized training. With mentoring, the conversation is typically shaped by the circumstances or tasks the mentee is facing. With formal trainings, there are key topics such as biblical foundations of the ministry, ministry values, discipleship principles, organizational structure, event planning strategies, and so much more that can be covered in a more systematic way. The teachings shared in such trainings have the potential to strengthen young leaders in the work of ministry, and we shouldn't cheat them out of this resource. There are four key outcomes a good training should seek to have.

1. **Alignment with the vision of the church.** In youth ministry, there is a natural rotation which occurs as youth age-in, grow, mature, and eventually age-out of our area of ministry. This rotation means that we need to continuously be sharing and teaching the vision of the church and our ministry. This is even more important for our leaders. Our ministry can quickly become divided if our young leaders do not understand why we do what we do. There is no end to the great ideas of how churches can reach out to the youth in their community, but not all of them will work for your church, and some of them will directly compete with other initiatives you are already invested in. Our trainings should include a time for sharing the vision of our church and helping our young leaders see the importance of being in alignment with it.

2. **Preparation for the work.** Youth ministry comes with many demands. The church has expectations, parents have expectations, and the youth themselves definitely have expectations. Without proper preparation for the work of youth ministry, young leaders will quickly find themselves chasing after ways to meet everyone's expectations without knowing how or not feeling the confidence to discern and establish their own priorities for the youth ministry. These trainings can help a young leader adjust to the realities of youth ministry and all it will require of them, while also equipping them to know how to respond to those challenges and the new challenges that will arise.

3. **Spiritual growth.** If our lessons are well considered, our young leaders should grow in their understanding of God and the ministry of the church in our world, as well as their understanding of the necessary practical skills. Spiritual matters such as prayer, discernment, and faith should be modeled and discussed during times of mentoring, however, these pieces should be reinforced through times of formal training. For example, lessons on event planning should Include times of prayer in the steps as a key part of our event preparation.

4. **Development of support relationships.** While mentoring is typically one-on-one, formal training is usually done with a group of people. During training sessions, our young leaders will get to know other leaders, hear their thoughts about ministry, share lessons learned, pray together, and intercede for one another. Working through such important issues together will often develop friendships that will last for the rest of their lives. These relationships will become a support system for our young leaders long after the formal training ends. In some ways they will sig-

nal a transition into peer mentoring. Therefore, it is important for our times of training to provide space for these types of relationships to form. If young leaders come, listen to one person talk, and then leave, it will be harder for these support relationships to take root.

5.   In his introductory comments to NYI's *Youth Ministry Training: 20 Foundational Lessons for Youth Ministry*, Dr. Dean Blevins writes, "One might argue that young people bring a visionary role to the church, often living and leading at the forefront of revival and church renewal throughout the history of Christianity. Providing sound leadership that both guides and empowers youth remains a crucial task for local congregations."' We must make space for this "crucial task."

Walking Side-by-Side

Whether we are mentoring or presenting a formal training, leadership development is strongest when we are walking side-by-side with our young leaders. Leadership can be very lonely. We can feel lost, without a path to follow, when problems arise in ministry. Even with personal problems, we can be overwhelmed if we don't know who we can share those struggles with. As leaders, we often carry a weight much heavier than what we should carry, and all while trying to be an example of Christian life and faith. However, if we are not careful, if we do not watch and pray and meditate on the Word daily, we may find ourselves in complicated situations without the support we need to make it through.

Modeling this humble and ministry-focused leadership teaches those we are mentoring how the strength of the ministry should be more important than our ego.

When we are developing young leaders, we need to share these hard truths with them as well as the fun, exciting dreams. As we walk side-by-side, we can share with them about the key people in our lives that support us. We can talk about how we prayerfully make difficult decisions. We can't use this as a time to disclose secrets of others in the church; out of respect, the confidentiality of others involved in difficult situations should be protected. However, we can share how we seek God and the wise counsel of others.

Walking side-by-side also allows us to share how we deal with our own weaknesses. We are not all gifted in all areas, and our ministry will be stronger when we are honest about our areas of weakness and seek out people with strengths in that area to balance out our ministry. Modeling this humble and ministry-focused leadership teaches those we are mentoring how the strength of the ministry should be more important than our ego. Share how you became aware of your own weaknesses and how you came to identify your strengths. Help young leaders explore these areas in a way that affirms who God created them to be and in no way makes them feel ashamed.

Finally, a key benefit to walking side-by-side with young leaders is how it will give you the confidence to know when they are ready to take on more responsibilities. In contrast to the model at the beginning of this chapter, such close walking together means you will have a front row seat to their growth and readiness for leadership. Seek out ways to include young leaders in youth ministry and hand off significant aspects of the ministry to them. Continue to walk beside them and mentor and encourage them, but don't manage their task for them. This approach calls us to do ministry with our youth, rather than for our youth. Eventually, we should encourage our young leaders to find even younger youth who they can begin to mentor. This is the cycle of leadership development and how we awaken the call of leadership in our youth and help them move from followers to leaders.

CHAPTER 5

Leading in the Local Church:
Making Space for Young Leaders to Grow

Cameron Batkin

Cameron Batkin is the Australia-New Zealand Field Youth Coordinator and serves in Hervey Bay, Australia. Youth ministry is exciting to him because he gets to witness young people come to God and grow in their faith. Cameron sees leadership development as an opportunity for young people to find their God-given gifts and talents and use them.

Before I jump into this chapter, I have to tell you that you have been on my mind and in my prayers for months. I was really excited to be invited to be part of this project because I believe in NYI, and I believe in our mission to share the hope of Jesus with young people. However, it is also true that you scare me to no end. I don't mean that personally, but you could be from any one of the over one hundred and sixty-two world areas where the Church of the Nazarene is at the time I am writing this. We so quickly forget about this great gift of our church. There are few denominations in as many world areas as we are with such a spirit of unity and connection. Still, it doesn't matter what continent you live on or how old you are, please know you are a vital and needed part of our church now and in the future. You stay in my prayers and I pray this book, and this chapter in particular, is a practical tool and a blessing to encourage you.

One more note: if you are anything like me, you read books in the voice of the author, or at least what you think the author sounds like. So for this chapter, you need to think of a mild Australian accent with not too much nasal buzz or twang. I like to think that I sound like Hugh Jackman; I just don't have the physique to match the voice.

I grew up in Inala, which is a suburb in the City of Brisbane, in the State of Queensland, in Australia. Inala was built post-World War II as an area to resettle returning soldiers. It was an area that also had a lot of government housing for the poor and those on government payments. It had a lot of negative social issues and had a very bad reputation in Brisbane for being a scary and violent place. My family was different, though. My dad worked in the railways, and we were buying our house. We lived just down the hill from a church, which is where, as a good child in the late 1970s, I was sent to Sunday School. It was, and still is, a Church of the Nazarene.

I wanted to start with a little of my background because in this chapter I will address leadership development as it is worked out in the local church. My own story is a perfect example of how the church can embrace this task. The local church is wonderfully diverse. It engenders deep emotions, both good and bad for many people. There have been times in my own life where I was frustrated and bored by ministry in the local church. I desired roles in more exciting places, like serving my district or going overseas on mission trips. It possibly took me too long to realise and actually understand the true beauty of the local church.

The local church is where we are able to get down to the heart of being the people of God in a specific place and share the love of God with the people of that specific community.

At the end of 2016, I was fortunate to attend the fourth National Youth Leaders Convention in Papua New Guinea. The Field Youth Coordinator, Daniel Latu, did a very cool session about the operational structure of NYI. It may sound like a bit of a bore, but trust me, Daniel was able to express it in a fun and practical way. He got various people out of the crowd to represent the various types of leadership in NYI. He had someone represent global NYI, then regional, field, district, and finally, the local church. It is very easy to look at the structure, see it rise upwards, and see global as the top of the journey. However, the beauty of our structure is that it is actually upside down. Everything we do is to feed, equip, and encourage the local church in its core mission of BE, DO, and GO.

The local church is where we are able to get down to the heart of being the people of God in a specific place and share the love of God with the people of that specific community. There is much beauty in the connectedness of our global denomination, but everything we do as a denomination is for the strength and support of our local churches and the communities they serve around the world. Conversely, our denomination depends on our local churches to raise up strong leaders who are committed to the work of God and the church. As youth workers, we have a significant role in the initial shaping of our young leaders, and the local church is a valuable partner for us in this endeavor.

A Local Beacon of Light

Matthew 5:14 says, "You are the light of the world. A town built on a hill cannot be hidden." Whenever I read this Scripture, my brain is automatically drawn to the local church I went to as a child. Our church was at the top of a hill and it was always easy to know if something was happening there. Above the door and the walls there was a full yellow glass front to the church. When the lights were on for youth group or juniors, it was very easy to see them from my front yard. Our church was quite literally a beacon on a hill. Likewise, through our actions and attitudes, the Body of Christ is to be a beacon of hope and love to our communities. I have been blessed over the years to be a part of local churches that have taken seriously their mission to share the hope and good news of Jesus with those all around. This is a contagious environment for young leaders to be drawn into and begin to dream about what God can do through the local church.

However, I am aware you might be reading this and thinking it is only possible for big churches, churches with massive staffs and teams of people to participate in and support significant outreach ministry. Well, please allow me to do some myth busting for you. In 2016, of the 29,335 reported local Churches of the Nazarene, 26,107, or 89%, had less than 100 people.[1] The Church of the Nazarene is doing significant work around the world, and it is based out of all sizes of congregations. God is not only working through the 11% of our churches with over 100 people, but God is using and wants to use us all. I know there are times in the local church when things are tough and repetitive, but be encouraged that the local church is the device God uses to help share the good news of Jesus. If it was not for my small local church (about 35 people), I could very surely say I would not be in the kingdom of God today.

As I described before, I went to Sunday School faithfully every time the doors were open. I was loved and embraced by some great leaders. I did it all, juniors and Vacation Bible School and really loved the Sunday School picnics. All of that was true until I was 10 years old. I was at Sunday School, and some boys from my grade at school followed me into a local hall. There were three or four of them, and they acted like pretty typical 10-year-old boys who were not used to Sunday School. They were noisy and rude and interrupted a lot. After the class, my teacher told me to never invite them back and that they were not welcome to come back again. I had accepted Jesus as my Saviour two years prior on junior camp, and even as a young Christian this sounded completely wrong. These were just the boys that needed to learn about God. I was deeply hurt by these comments and refused to go to Sunday School again.

When I was 12, I was invited to the youth group the church ran on Friday nights by one of my closest friends in the neighbourhood. She wasn't a

Christian but had started going. She told me youth group was OK but that they talked about God a lot. I was not surprised as that is what a church is supposed to do. It sounded better than sitting around home with my parents, so I went. I spent the next three years watching them intently and checking them out to see if they were the real deal. They were. They coped with the pressure and turmoil of life in a way I could not imagine. They showed me how their faith was a vital and real part of their lives. Their lives were not all sunshine and flowers, but their faith did have a big impact on them for the better.

The summer I was 16, I went to the district camp, and I asked God into my life, to forgive my sins and to change me. Simultaneously, that is where my journey into leadership began. We had five teens in our youth group, and at that summer camp, four of the five of us came to Christ. Our pastor's wife started leading the youth group and the four of us were brought into a discipleship group. The four of us also became the youth council with the tasks of serving the youth group. My journey into leadership had begun, even if I didn't know it at the time.

Making Space for Young Leaders to Grow

Our pastor and his wife taught us from very early on how vital it was to our discipleship to serve others in a practical way in addition to learning and growing in our relationship with God. Those four young men were and are, to this day, very different people. Some are great with their hands, some are musically talented, some can sing, while others are not encouraged to sing as much. But we were encouraged to bring our unique gifts and to be united together as part of the Body of Christ.

When we approach youth ministry as something we do for youth, we rob them of the chance to learn at a young age what it means to offer all of themselves to God for His church. Youth ministry should be something we do with youth, making space for them to grow and develop as leaders. When we planned activities as a youth council, we would plan out the schedule, meet together to set out the terms, and take turns overseeing the various responsibilities needed for the activity to happen. We would take turns in leading games, running the prayer time and leading the devotions. This was a very big time of learning and making mistakes. We learnt very quickly how things often do not go as planned. We learnt just how quickly we could make big mistakes. The adults around us made space for us to have an atmosphere and culture of trust which could not be broken, and it gave us the courage to try.

This is really important to learn; our young people can be intimidated by our perceived perfection or inability to admit when we are wrong. Learning to admit when I am wrong and asking for forgiveness from those I have wronged was one of the most liberating things I learnt in the journey of being a leader. I had falsely accused one of our young people of something one week. After making amends for the situation, I was driving one of his friend's home when he said to me, "I could never see myself as a Christian because I thought you had to be perfect, but now I realise that you don't have to be perfect all of the time."

> **When we approach youth ministry as something we do for youth, we rob them of the chance to learn at a young age what it means to offer all of themselves to God for His church.**

Nonetheless, we don't just let our youth fail. I think debriefing is always important in ministry, but especially when younger leaders are learning new skills. Part of our process while packing up after youth group was making the time to have even a very short time of feedback and prayer as a team. We would continue to grow through the shared experiences that we would have together.

Making space for young leaders to grow takes intentionality and often will take more work. However, it is important for us to remember that our goal is not to have a perfectly run youth group, but rather to raise up young believers who know and value their God-given gifts and see the importance of using those gifts for the work of God.

Fostering Growth in Young Leaders

One of the questions often asked in leadership development is whether or not leadership development is for everyone. I would wholeheartedly say, yes! As I mentioned previously, going through the journey of learning what it meant to be a leader was a huge part of my discipleship. It helped me to grow and express what I was reading in the Scriptures and learning in prayer. I think it also helped me define what a leader is. When we see the word "leader," we think of someone in power, someone who has a lot of control. I know this definition will change dramatically from culture to culture, however, I think one of the gifts we offer to the young people in the church is to help them redefine leadership according to God's view of leadership, rather than the predominant cultural definition. If we think of a leader as a person of influence, that definition is much broader than what we think of when we normally think of a leader. Along with a new understanding of leadership, we will help youth be able to see themselves as leaders. This will empower them to embrace their God-given gifts and talents and allow us to come alongside them and foster their growth as leaders. I believe we can foster growth in young leaders by giving attention to self-leadership, gifts and talents, responsibility, self-awareness, and the development of new skills.

Self-Leadership

The first gift we can give our young people is the tool of self-leadership. This is a good foundation on which to build the other skills. It is the simple issues like time management, handling responsibility, and showing respect to others. In my culture at least, it is seen that is hard to lead others if you can't get to a meeting on time, prepare yourself for a devotion, or perform some other task. You already read a whole chapter on self-leadership earlier in this book, but I encourage you to take these principles and help your youth incorporate them into their lives and leadership practices as well.

Gifts and Talents

When we see the term leader, we usually think of someone who is up front and seen by people. However, leadership is much broader. What is seen up front is such a small part of all the Kingdom work being done for the church to grow and flourish. If we didn't have leaders who took care of the administration and finances of the church, we would quickly find our work hindered by problems. If we didn't have people with the skills to help provide food or oversee the technical aspects of the church, our outreach efforts would lack those meaningful components.

As we began to develop a leadership team with our youth, we provided a spiritual gifts inventory for them to participate in. This helped us look at the gifts God had given them for service to the church and others. It is easy for us to take our skills for granted and assume everyone can do the same things. These inventories can be very useful in helping youth take their talents seriously. Many spiritual gifts inventories are available online. While they are helpful, they do not replace the guidance of the Holy Spirit. Whether you use these inventories or not, draw spiritual leaders from your church into the process. Look up the passages in the Bible that discuss the various spiritual gifts, and set aside a time of prayer and discernment. Invite several spiritual leaders in the church to get to know and observe the youth on your leadership team. Use this as a time of discernment and then affirmation of the various talents observed in your youth.

Responsibility

While we are recruiting young people to be a part of the leadership team and bringing them on this journey of learning to be a leader, we found it was critical to set expectations. I know many ministries have their volunteers and young leaders enter into covenants or contracts. I think these can be great tools to set fair expectations as to what is expected of the younger leaders especially. One of the things we are teaching our younger leaders is responsibility. It can often be very easy for people to cancel at the last minute and go do something more exciting. We live in a time where FOMO (Fear of Missing Out) is alive and rampant, not just in our young people but in people of all ages. I think these contracts and covenants need to be written together as a team, with individuals focused on the church perspective but with the opinions of the young leaders as well. If they are one-sided, they can be seen very negatively and very quickly young people will feel like they are being forced into something. Ministry in all its forms is something to be relished and enjoyed, not something that you are coerced and forced into.

Self-Awareness

There are many different tools available to help individuals grow in the area of self-awareness. One tool we've used is the Myers-Briggs temperament sorter. It is a great tool to help us identify how we relate with others and how our personality can impact our style of leadership. In general, this test shows us how we will typically respond to different situations or pressures, and it can help us be aware of those tendencies and make sure our response is intentional, not just instinctual. An example is that one trait my type is known for is being so focused on the task or the goal that we do not consider the views or the needs of others we work with or are working for. Being aware of this tendency has helped me in crucial times. Find ways to help your young leaders think intentionally about who they are, how they respond, and how they can be more intentional.

Develop New Skills

A fundamental part of growing as a leader is developing new skills. Some skills will come more naturally than others, but it doesn't mean we should only do what we already know how to do. Some say we should build up your strengths, but I think an awareness of our weaknesses is also beneficial. It is an important part of learning and growth to try things that are not our natural talent. Especially for our young leaders who are still developing in so many areas, it is important for us to help them try new things. Once we see someone is really good in one area, it is a big temptation to want to assign them there so we don't have to worry about it. However, our young leaders need the chance to explore.

The Natural Strength of the Small, Local Church

Something I have come to appreciate from my discipleship and leadership training in a smaller church was the unity of our church life. One of the greatest crimes committed against the church is the growth of age-appropriate ministries with the children over in one space, the youth in another, and both kept as separate as possible from the senior adults. When we look at 1 Corinthians 12:12, the first thing to jump out at me about the Body of Christ is that there is no mention of age. I am not exactly sure why we do it, but it is not scriptural or beneficial to the body.

> **One of the greatest crimes committed against the church is the growth of age-appropriate ministries with the children over in one space, the youth in another, and both kept as separate as possible from the senior adults.**

We need as much unity as possible and more opportunities to be together, rather than apart. There is much that we can learn from each other if we just took the time to stop and listen to each other. In over twenty years of working with young people, one of the scariest things we've ever done was take a group of Polynesian young people three hours into the country to visit with a nursing home full of elderly farmers. From the outset, you could feel the tension from both groups. We encouraged our young people to ask questions about unifying topics and about what life was like for these farmers as teenagers. The encounter changed very quickly, as our young people held onto every slow and deliberate word uttered. We finished with some Christmas carols in Samoan. In the end, it was very hard to get our kids out of there, which was the direct opposite from just an hour and a half before.

When our young people encounter the older members of our congregations, we forget that to become old, one first had to be young. We need to create as many opportunities as possible to share life together. This need for unity applies to the connection between children and youth as well. Another blessing of my ministry was the time I spent teaching Sunday School and ultimately becoming a Sunday School superintendent at the age of 19. Children love the opportunity to hang out with teens and often see them as something aspirational. Many children cannot wait to be teens and to enjoy all the freedoms they perceive come with being a bit older. Having our teens serve in the children's ministry is significant for our children, but it also helps our youth learn what it is like to be a role model and share their faith with others.

Whether you are in a small church or a large church, the local church is a natural place to help youth develop as leaders; we just need to be intentional about how we think about leadership and how we include youth in what we do. As you enter this journey of leadership development, I pray this chapter has been helpful and useful. Above all, remember your foundation is found in prayer. Pray for God to bring you young people willing to grow in his love and learn how to be a leader. In this journey, make sure they have role models who foster personal growth, opportunities to learn new skills, and a supportive environment where they can make mistakes along the way. Help them use whatever tools are available to discover their gifts and talents and about their personality so they develop open, dynamic teams bound together by God's love and the church's trust in them. We want our young people to know they are a vital part of the Body of Christ, made up of all ages.

CHAPTER 6

Leadership Communities:
Growing and Learning Alongside One Another

Phil Starr

Phil Starr is the pastor of student ministries at Lima Community Church and serves in Lima, Ohio, United States. Youth ministry is exciting to him because teens are still developing, and many experiences have a touch of novelty and discovery. Leadership development is import-ant to Phil because it creates a culture where people can feel empowered to dream, practice, and influence others as they grow.

Developing Leadership Communities that 'GO'

I am not a fan of the Tour De France. However, one must admire the efficiency and concentration required of the cyclists as they navigate the carbon frame through the French countryside, towns, and mountains. Many of the cyclists remain in pace-lines, keeping the front tire within a couple inches from the preceding cyclist. As the race progresses, the pace-line strategy must be taken seriously. "Cyclists who are part of the group can save up to 40 percent in energy expenditures over a cyclist who is not drafting with the group. To be effective drafting, a cyclist needs to be as close as possible to the bicycle in front of him."[1] During the race, exhausted cyclists begin falling out of faster pace-lines. As cyclists fall out of pace-lines, commentators begin debating on the possibility of the cyclist returning to the pace-line. Then there are the wrecks. Choosing to ride in a pace-line entails a couple of realities. First, when you ride close together, you win together. Second, when you ride close together, you wreck together. There isn't a better example of this than the 2007 Tour De France. During the final moments of stage two, a surprise movement of a rider led to a colossal pile up hindering a speedy, sprint-filled finish by many. Despite the risk of injury, cyclists know a basic truth: you go further and faster when you ride together.

The same is true about leadership.

Leaders have moments when we must stand alone as decision makers, leading others towards a particular outcome. Nevertheless, standing alone as a leader is not the same as living in isolation. Anyone who has had the responsibility to lead a school project group, organize an event, or mobilize people understands the weight of making decisions. It isn't always easy making decisions, especially when they lead us into a direction of unknown territory. If hindsight is 20/20 or perfect vision, then foresight into the future is unguaranteed and cloudy at best. Then there comes the moment of clarity, which brings responsibility. In this clarity we see the results of our decision and must own the consequences — both the mistakes and the successes. These are lonely places, even for seasoned leaders. Imagine the insecurities, fears, and vulnerabilities that exist for the developing teen leader. Their longings could include a desire for a safe place to fail. Is there a place where they are able to test and question their concepts before actually making a final decision? Is there a place where they can find confidence from others when they are struggling to find it within themselves? The answers to these questions are found in community. Henri Nouwen writes, "In community we say: 'Life is full of gains and losses, joys and sorrows, ups and downs — but we do not have to live it alone.'"[2]

Developing leaders who will GO bids one to become intentional developers of leadership communities.

We as youth leaders long to find those two or three passionate teen leaders. It almost seems to be a rare blessing if one is able to experience the joy of a teen leader at least once during their ministry at a specific church. The rarity of finding teen leaders might have to do more with a leader's process of developing leaders than presence of potential leaders. Again, it is possible that the challenge of developing leaders is more connected to the process we youth leaders use than the actual presence of potential leaders. The process of building leadership communities allows us to create environments for teen leaders to discover personal growth and practice leadership.

Here are some thoughts on community:

The Christian community is a living testimony whose confession includes the far-reaching and inclusive availability of God's promise of hope in Jesus. Creating leadership communities allows for an inclusive space for teens of many different leadership styles and passions to find belonging, purpose, and experience. A non-negotiable truth of community is this: *experiencing community requires effort.* This is one of the reasons youth pastors sometimes neglect even the idea of building a leadership group of teens — whether the group contains 3 or 150 youth. Youth leaders, with their typically busy schedules of planning programs, work, family, caring for people, and maintaining the demands of the church, are overburdened and exhausted. They want teen leaders and agree there are benefits of such peer leadership; nevertheless, the requirement of hours needed to develop a highly assertive and focused teen is comparatively less than developing a community of teen leaders. Abraham Joshua Heschel, a renowned Jewish Rabbi and teacher of Jewish philosophy, describes, "Man is a seeker after the greatest degree of comfort for the least necessary expenditure of energy."[3] Leaders can fall into this tendency of fulfilling a desire for a beneficial component of their ministries by only soliciting the "loudest" and "most available" teens for leadership.

Only appealing to the "loud" and "most easily available" is a trap for ministries. It is a trap that produces shallow and often narrow influence even though the attendance creates an illusion of deep leadership development. Time is required by the leader to develop a community of teen leaders. There will be sacrifices of the normal ministry requirements. The weekly routine will have to be adjusted. Building community among leaders doesn't come easy, but it is a must.

Let's return to the Tour De France picture of community.

Imagine if the leadership development within youth ministries resembled more of a cyclist's pace-line rather than a classroom? The developer or leader would act less like an expert of facts and predictor of outcomes and more like a trainer who prepares the community to work together and rotate through leadership experiences. Imagine if teens were given opportunities to experience success, failure, problem solving, and even possibly injury — to both ego and body. The trainer transforms into one who treats wounds, celebrates wins, reminds the team of the finish line, teaches fundamentals, and cares for their soul.

Seeing a community of teens discover the joy of Christian leadership is life-giving.

At the end of the day, the teens who participate in such a community are able to experience what it is like to take their turn at leading the pack with the confidence of their trainer/leader. Each teen leader learns the hard lessons of focus, concentration, boundaries, and responsibility. Failure and underperformance become beautiful because the community crashes together. The wins are even more captivating because they win together, and by going together, they go further. Even more desirable — in the community of leaders, youth leaders become shepherds again.

Building community and developing teen leaders can be exhausting. Seeing a community of teens discover the joy of Christian leadership is life-giving.

Hopefully you have bought into the importance of creating leadership communities. What follows are some of the processes youth leaders on my region are using to develop leaders.

Apprenticeships

A youth pastor who has been in ministry for 20 years explained his complete frustration with student leadership development. After going through different leadership books and workshops, he became disillusioned with leadership programs. The programs did not match his context. The programs may have worked for one generation but not for the next. The pursuit of the program model eventually led into an apprenticeship model.

This model of leadership development focuses on building leadership communities with current leaders rather than a group of new students. Many times, these leaders are seasoned adults. The youth leader discovers a teen with a potential talent or passion and then matches each student leader to a specific adult. The role of the adult is to focus on building a relationship and teaching skill competency.

An example of this is the teen who wants to learn how to operate the sound system. The youth leader identifies a teen that is interested in learning. The teen is connected to an adult who is already operating the sound system. They are taught the fundamentals of being responsible, given ownership of a ministry need, and experience the successes/mistakes of technology. Other areas of examples include class teachers for children, ushering, greeting, preaching, serving, and planning. In reality, the possibilities are endless with the right amount of creativity.

This model has the benefit of sharing the responsibility of leadership development with other leaders. The youth leader isn't required to teach each teen the details of their leadership roles because other adults are focusing on specific interests and teaching individual teens. Having other adults involved in teens' lives also connects youth to other generations. This protects our ministries from becoming a closed group based on specific ages. A teen that has committed to becoming an apprentice soon sees how they are an essential part of their church family.

The apprentice model is enhanced when the youth leader can help the seasoned adult catch a vision for discipling their assigned teen. Imagine if the task of ministry was just an excuse to participate in the spiritual formation of another person. An easy way of beginning this kind of awareness is to encourage the teen and seasoned adult to ask each other only three questions each time they are together. "How was your week?" "Where have you seen God this week?" "How can I pray for you this week?" These intentional questions strengthen relationships and provide pathways for teaching truth.

The apprentice relationship also provides an opportunity for testimony. Stories give us context to discover God and ourselves. Even though biblical stories are highly significant, the contemporary testimony of an older Christian provides a living story in which to see Jesus.

There are a couple of mistakes that can happen with the apprentice model. One of the mistakes is focusing more on the activity or skill than the heart. The most important truth a teen needs to take away from leadership is their identity in Jesus, rather than skill competence. Another mistake is when the youth leader loses touch with the young leader or fails to connect the teen to their peer community. Apprenticeship is a great way of sharing the responsibility, but it is not abandoning responsibility. Youth leaders must stay engaged, at some level, with their young leaders.

Overall, the apprentice model strengthens some of the weak spots of typical youth ministries. Here we recognize that leadership communities are not limited to a single generation. Thriving leadership communities involve the knowledge, participation, and testimony of the old and young. Youth leaders can capitalize on specific ministry skills as a means to spiritually disciple others.

Student Ministry Team

Another youth leader who has been in ministry for over 15 years has noticed a common byproduct of leadership teams — an arrogant and elitist attitude.

It is common for youth leaders on my region to transition churches throughout their ministry as youth leaders. Upon arriving at a new ministry assignment, this particular youth leader noticed how the current student leaders saw themselves as the aristocracy of the youth group. Rather than abandoning the idea of student leadership, he decided to change the name from "Student Leadership Team" to "Student Ministry Team" therefore emphasizing serving others over leadership.

Unlike the apprentice model, the student ministry team is a well-developed process. It includes an entry point, specific teachings, assigned homework, and ministry responsibilities. The ministry team finds its identity in Matthew 20:26, "…whoever wants to become great among you must be your servant."

The student ministry team is open for anyone who is willing to be a part of the community. There isn't an application process, but there are expectations. Some of the expectations include participating in regular meetings, selecting a ministry area in which to serve, and a monetary fee to cover a t-shirt. The all-inclusive mentality creates a community where teens are welcome to discover their specific leadership styles and passions. Inclusivity recognizes the value of diversity while emphasizing the common purpose of serving others.

The student ministry team meets after school once a week as a group with the youth leader. During this time, the youth leader teaches through specific subjects of servant leadership. Topics are dictated by various Scripture studies from the book of Matthew. Each student begins with his or her testimony, goes through the Sermon on the Mount, and ends with the great commission. Teens are expected to memorize correlating Scripture.

The student ministry team also commits to individual and communal practices. For instance, during a specific month, a teen might make a personal commitment to fast. Other individual practices include tithing, praying, devotions, evangelism, and serving. During the same month, the group might commit to the communal practice of accountability with one another. These personal and collective practices help to foster growth, commitment, and community. Other communal practices include teaching others, serving the marginalized, and participating in sacraments. The culture of the community transforms from elitism to growing and going together.

The student ministry team connects their learning times to specific ministry commitments during the week. Each teen is expected to commit to a ministry role within their youth ministry or church ministry. Some of these roles include planning, helping with tasks, and hospitality.

One of the advantages of the student ministry team is the emphasis on serving others. Too many times a great leadership model has been jeopardized by pride and exclusiveness. Right from the beginning, this model emphasizes the teaching of Jesus to serve others. The reward of the teen comes from a common desire to please our Savior, rather than a desire to be recognized.

The identity of the student leader is inseparable from the identity of the group. This particular youth leader does well in emphasizing communal responsibility and dependence. Not only are the values taught, but the group must make a collective commitment to regularly practicing formational activities together.

It is important to remain intentional with creating pathways for other adults and leaders to influence student leaders. It is really easy for a youth leader to take the responsibility of developing a student ministry team upon himself or herself. The formation of the leadership community would not thrive without the influence of a broad group of Christian leaders. The youth leader might also suffer from exhaustion or fall into the habit of cancelling weekly meetings when an unplanned situation requires his or her attention.

Generally, the student ministry team highlights the need for proper teaching and consistent gathering to form leadership communities. The curriculum is developed from the Gospel of Matthew, and students are taught to engage Scripture as they serve. The ministry team takes work and consistency, but the result is more than just skills; it is a development of student identity.

Leadership Conversations

Busyness seems to be common to all cultures. The numerous distractions of our surroundings are making it increasingly difficult to find common times to develop students in community. After becoming frustrated with the common excuse of "I can't meet that day," a couple youth leaders decided to focus on having regular leadership conversations rather than initiating a complex program.

Twice a month, after the Sunday night youth program, the youth leaders meet with a group of teens to talk about leadership principles. The length of the conversation ranges from 10 to 15 minutes. The short conversations are based on popular leadership books. Each of the conversations walks through the following three steps. First, the specific leadership principle is shared through a short teaching or common reading. Secondly, teens are asked how each unique principle applies to their contexts of leadership. Finally, the group ends with prayer. Once a month, during the same specific time, the group discusses their relationship with God and shares how they are maintaining connectedness to God and each other.

The youth leaders personally invite the teens involved in the leadership conversations. There isn't an application process or open invitation. This maintains a continual development of the youth ministry's core students. The freedom of the conversations allows the leaders to tailor the topics to best create growth in the teens.

The concept of teens joining a community that takes seriously the necessity of growing and serving creates a safe place for teens to share successes and mistakes that might typically be overlooked in models focused on church ministries.

One of the benefits of this model is the recognition of the different leadership contexts. In some of the other models, the leadership context tends to emphasize church activities as the primary place to utilize leadership skills. In most cases, teens involved in church leadership are exhibiting the same leadership characteristics in their schools, clubs, families, and sports. The conversational model engages these other contexts as areas of influence. The teens are challenged to grow and go serve as a leader in all of their areas of influence.

This model also intentionally makes the effort to combine spiritual formation and leadership formation as a focus of the community. The concept of teens joining a community that takes seriously the necessity of growing and serving creates a safe place for teens to share successes and mistakes that might typically be overlooked in models focused on church ministries. The culture becomes a common commitment to confess, encourage, and empower one another.

As a word of caution, the personal invitation process creates the possibility for this model to overlook future teen leaders. This will happen if the youth leader is the only means of identifying leadership candidates and they default to inviting only the teens they know best. One might also question the role of other leaders in the formation of teen leaders. We must make sure other adults are connecting with these young leaders in order to create a greater community where these teens are connected.

This model can be celebrated in its relentless pursuit to develop leadership communities amid a busy world. The shortness of time can appear as a shallow attempt of speaking into teens' lives, however, the consistent participation of teens and the youth leaders builds a culture of leadership, which goes beyond the church ministry.

Leadership Community

A youth leader explained to me their struggle to find the right teens to develop as a leadership team. First, there were parents who challenged the youth leaders' expectations of the teens, calling them "unrealistic" and "worthy of a discussion with the senior pastor." Secondly, there were teens who were invited to lead because of their availability but who were not committed to leading. Both cases led to a community of teens that lacked commitment to growing and serving together. These experiences led the youth leader to begin forming a leadership community that involved regular meetings, foundational teachings, activities of service, and an entry process for teens desiring to grow as leaders.

All teens in the youth ministry, both new teens from the community and teens that had grown up in the church, are given an open invite into the leadership community. The open invite is paired with very clear expectations. The following expectations are required of each student before joining the leadership community. Students must complete 20 service hours from activities beyond church ministry and missions. Students must memorize eight Bible verses. Students must express their commitment to their youth ministry through regular attendance patterns. Finally, the expectations must be approved and signed by a parent or guardian. These expectations are annual requirements for both new and returning teens.

The kickoff event was a leadership weekend retreat focused on the heart and hands of leadership. The retreat was kept simple and inexpensive. It utilized the teachings of Leadertreks, a youth ministry leadership organization that provides curriculum and ideas on developing teen leaders. Even though the leadership retreat is emphasized as the ideal time to join the community, teens are welcomed to join throughout the year as long as they are fulfilling the expectations.

The leadership community continues to meet bi-monthly for learning and a meal. The meetings continue to cover leadership principles. Each meeting focuses on three distinct areas of leadership — teamwork, the character of a leader, and the acts of leadership. The meeting ends with the teens creating and planning a group service project. The meal was added for those desiring to build community beyond the teaching.

The leadership team plans two service projects for the youth ministry each year. These service projects range from landscaping at local nursing homes to serving food to local refugees and leading VBS programs. The teens are expected to plan and lead with the adults playing supporting roles. The youth leader explained the joy of seeing his teen leaders executing a VBS program during an international mission trip. The adults and missionaries were impressed.

This model creates an atmosphere of high expectations. Spiritual formation, the ability to work well with each other, and leadership are identified as equally important parts of growing and going together. The leadership community model accentuates the value of faith-based communities in a culture that expects very little from typical faith-based communities. However, the high expectations can also lead to very limited teen participation. The regular meetings and service hours required eliminate teens that are navigating busy schedules. Teens who might not have a strong support structure at home will also require additional help from youth leaders in order to accomplish the service hours. It is important for leadership communities to include both the resourced and the resource-challenged demographics of the culture.

By and large, this model requires us to ask ourselves if we are creating programs of commitment and expectation. Built into this model are communal practices of creating ownership and responsibility. Teens aren't expected to lead in places of comfort but are stretched through additional tasks. It highlights inclusiveness with a balance of requiring individual effort.

In looking at how many youth leaders are creating leadership communities in their youth ministry, I couldn't help but notice how many of the great ideas resulted from moments of failure and frustration. This reality is a source of positive encouragement for youth leaders. Leadership communities can be developed. This positive mindset arrives not only from others' stories, but also the realization of other common dynamics that exists in our communities.

Final Thoughts

Youth leaders, do not become discouraged when the season of strong leaders are replaced by young and new potential leaders. Youth ministry is a birthing ministry of discipling teens and parents during a specific season of life. There is an entry point and exit point. Efforts to develop leaders might bear more fruit or less fruit depending on the season of the ministry. The changing of ministry seasons isn't necessarily a sign of poor leadership or bad parenting. People are different and respond differently to programs and plans.

Because there are different seasons in ministry, it is important for us to also admit that it might be time to change our strategy. This might be a time to replace a highly demanding leadership program with a more relational, conversational model. For the youth leader who has transitioned from one ministry assignment location to another, the cultural context of the community plays an important role in deciding what model may or may not be suitable for developing leadership communities.

Creating leadership communities where teens can grow and serve together takes effort. It is a birthing process that mourns teens who decide to say no to leadership, sends teens to lead beyond their season of adolescence, and welcomes goofy new teens into the journey of serving and influencing others.

Another important note to remember is that apathy and lack of commitment exist in all cultures. We naturally tend to focus on ourselves, and we won't always choose pathways of taking responsibility and serving others. Some of our most loved teens, even though they admire the idea of becoming a leader, won't have the commitment. Even worse, some of our most potential leaders don't have a desire to participate in a leadership community. Communities suffer when teens cease to be involved and committed. Teens suffer as well. However, youth leaders must focus on leading those who follow while also mourning those we love.

Creating leadership communities where teens can grow and serve together takes effort. It is a birthing process that mourns teens who decide to say no to leadership, sends teens to lead beyond their season of adolescence, and welcomes goofy new teens into the journey of serving and influencing others. Developing communities where imperfect people experience grace and truth demands diligence and grit, and the result is worth the work. Leadership communities become places to discover how the act of leading is connected to a right relationship with Jesus. In community, we discover the diversity of leadership instead of mistakenly raising specific styles and roles to a place of honor.

Leaders GO further and grow deeper together.

Rene Vietto is a legend among the Tour De France. One of his stories involved an amputated toe in order to save weight. (I will let you decide the truth of that story.) Rene Vietto was a hotel busboy turned professional cyclist for the French team. His initial role on the team was that of a "servant" to the team captain. It was his job to help his team, specifically his leader, stay strong and win. His responsibilities included providing pace support and helping with wrecks. During a mountain climbing stage of the Tour De Fance, his leader, Antonin Magne, had an accident. Vietto had pulled ahead of all but one of his teammates among the mountains. As he was racing, the team's motorcade informed him of his leader's accident, which had badly damaged Magne's bicycle. Vietto could have easily continued, expecting his other teammates to stop and help. However, what followed was remarkable. Vietto turned around, travelling back through the two mountain passes he had just traversed. Upon finding Magne, he gave his bike to the leader and waited for the support team to provide him with another bicycle for the race. Magne, with Vietto's bicycle, managed to win the race and the 1934 Tour De France.

Rene Vietto's commitment to his team is a picture of the type of leaders our ministries desire to develop. These are leaders who are selfless servants, committed to the mission of the community, sacrificing everything to GO together for the hope of Jesus.

WORKS CITED/NOTES

Introduction

1. Hammond, Kim, Darren Cronshaw. *Sentness: Six Postures of Missional Christians.* IVP Books, 2014.

2. Wright, N. T. *The Day the Revolution Began: Reconsidering the Meaning of Jesus's Crucifixion* [Kindle Edition]. HarperCollins, 2016.
   "The vocation in question is that of being a genuine human being, with genuinely human tasks to perform as part of the Creator's purpose for his world. The main task of this vocation is "image-bearing," reflecting the Creator's wise stewardship into the world and reflecting the praises of all creation back to its maker."

3. Sweet, Leonard. *I Am a Follower: The Way, Truth, and Life of Following Jesus* [Kindle Edition]. Thomas Nelson, 2012.
   "We have been told our entire lives that we should be leaders, that we need more leaders, leaders, leaders. But the truth is that the greatest way to create a movement is to be a follower and to show others how to follow. Following is the most underrated form of leadership in existence."

Chapter 1

1. Wolinski, Steve. "Leadership Defined." *Managementhelp.org*, managementhelp.org/blogs/leadership/2010/04/06/leadership-defined. 30 March 2017.

2. Munroe, Myles. *The Spirit of Leadership.* Whitaker House, 2005.

3. McKenna, Amy. *The 100 Most Influential World Leaders of All Time.* Britannica Educational Pub., 2010.

4. "What Is Servant Leadership?" *Greenleaf.org*, www.greenleaf.org/what-is-servant-leadership. 2016.

5. Abingdon Press. *The New Interpreter's Dictionary of the Bible.* Abingdon Press, 2006.

Chapter 2

1. Bullón, Dorothy. "El avivamiento que cambió un país: Una mirada de Inglaterra antes y después del Gran Avivamiento del siglo XVIII." *Wesley.nnu.edu*, wesley.nnu.edu/fileadmin/imported_site/espanol/El_avivamiernto_que_cambio_un_pais.pdf. 21 November 2013.

2. Ortíz, Félix, Annette Gulick, Gerardo Muniello. *Raíces: Pastoral juvenil en profundidad.* Editorial Vida, 2008.

3. Moody, William R. *D. L. Moody*. The MacMillan Company, 1930.

4. Gay, Milton. *Plan de Vuelo*. Casa Nazarena de Publicaciones, 2013.

5. Ortiz, Félix. *Liderazgo Personal: 9 Herramientas prácticas para alcanzar tu potencial*. Aragon Books, 2016.

Chapter 3

1. These resources can be found online at growingleaders.com/habitudes.

2. Elmore, Tim. *Habitudes Book #1: The Art of Self-Leadership*. Growing Leaders, Inc., 2013.

Chapter 4

1. Blevins, Dean. "Youth Ministry Training: 20 Foundational Lessons for Youth Ministry." *Whdl.org*, www.whdl.org/collections/youth-ministry-training-20-foundational-les-sons-youth-ministry.

Chapter 5

1. "General secretary releases 2016 stats." *Nazarene.org*, www.nazarene.org/article/gener-al-secretary-releases-2016-stats. 8 December 2016.

Chapter 6

1. "Aerodynamics." *Exploratorium.edu*, www.exploratorium.edu/cycling/aerodynamics2.html. 28 April 2017.

2. Nouwen, Henri J.M., Wendy Wilson Greer. *The Only Necessary Thing: Living a Prayerful Life*. Claretian Publications, 2004.

3. Heschel, Abraham J. *Who Is Man?* Stanford University Press, 1995.

CPSIA information can be obtained
at www.ICGtesting.com
Printed in the USA
FSHW010306130321
79455FS